BBC Books, an imprint of Ebury Publishing
20 Vauxhall Bridge Road, London SW1V 2SA

BBC Books is part of the Penguin Random House group of companies
whose addresses can be found at global.penguinrandomhouse.com

Penguin
Random House
UK

Text by Christian Guiltenane
Cover and book design: Clarkevanmeurs Design

This book is published to accompany the television series
RuPaul's Drag Race UK, a World of Wonder production for BBC Three

www.penguin.co.uk

A CIP catalogue record for this book is available from the British Library

ISBN 9781785946417

Publishing Director: Albert DePetrillo
Commissioning Editor: Yvonne Jacob
Project Editor: Daniel Sørensen
Production: Sian Pratley

Printed and bound in Great Britain by Bell and Bain Ltd, Glasgow

The authorised representative in the EEA is Penguin Random House
Ireland, Morrison Chambers, 32 Nassau Street, Dublin D02 YH68

Penguin Random House is committed to a sustainable future for
our business, our readers and our planet. This book is made
from Forest Stewardship Council® certified paper.

Contents

MEET THIS YEAR'S QUEENS

Veronica Green	22
Ella Vaday	32
Elektra Fence	40
Kitty Scott-Claus	48
Vanity Milan	66
Anubis	78
Choriza May	84
Scarlett Harlet	92
Krystal Versace	100
River Medway	106
Charity Kase	116
Victoria Scone	122

MINI CHALLENGES

Choose Your Drag Name	26
Drag Race UK Translations	82
Drag Race Bingo	90
The Charisma, Uniqueness, Nerve and Talent Quiz	104
She Said What?	114
The Queen Of The Queens Quiz	120
You Better Word Search	126

MAXI FEATURES

Welcome to Ru's World   8

**Bring Back My Girls,
A History: Part 1**   18

The Library is Open!   28

**Super Heroes Assemble:
Drag Origins**   36

**The *Drag Race UK*
Hall Of Fame**   52

***Drag Race* Saved My Life**   58

**Bring Back My Girls,
A History: Part 2**   62

The Snatch Game Secrets   96

World Of Wonder   110

EXCLUSIVE INTERVIEWS

**How's Your Head, Hun?
A foreword from
Michelle Visage**   6

**You're A Winner Baby!
Lawrence Chaney**   12

**You're A Winner Baby!
The Vivienne**   16

**Not A Joke. Just A Fact.
Bimini Bon-Boulash**   44

Spill the Tia! Tia Kofi   70

**How To Make Your Life
Much Better. Baga Chipz**   74

**At Home With A'Whora
And Tayce**   88

How's your head, hun?

A foreword from

Michelle Visage

Hello, baby dolls, it's Michelle Visage, and welcome to the first ever *RuPaul's Drag Race UK* annual.

Now, I really hope you've enjoyed season three – it's just been wonderful, hasn't it? Like the previous two, we've got to meet so many brilliant, amazing, larger-than-life characters, who you will get to know even better throughout this fabulous book.

As much as I adore the American version of *Drag Race* I have to admit I am particularly fond of the Brit series. You see, for many years, the UK has had a big place in my heart and has become like a second home to me.

I cannot tell you how pleased I am that it has gone on to become the huge global success it has. I mean, everybody's talking about it. Just everybody! Not that I'm surprised, of course! I always knew it would be a runaway success, because when the American series first aired, the largest fan base outside of the States was you guys, the United Kingdolls.

When the first series of *Drag Race UK* aired back in 2019, I felt like a proud mom and have continued to do so ever since. The success of the series has really proven that everybody likes drag. I mean, what's not to love? Drag is cool. Drag is art. I mean, who feels ashamed to say they like Britney Spears or the Spice Girls? So why would you be ashamed to say you like drag?

What *Drag Race* UK does is showcase that there is a type of drag for absolutely everybody. It's not just about being beautiful or having your make-up being perfectly blended. It's about expression. Some people do it with scary make-up, like Charity Kase. Some people do it through costuming – it's an incredible viable art form that's been around

forever and will be here long after *Drag Race*.

We're living in a great time during which we have seen drag culture evolve. When *Drag Race* started in the US, we were in a totally different place and we had a totally different vision and now it has taken the world by storm and I think everybody understands what drag is really about.

I mean, I've always considered myself a drag queen. I even have a huge tattoo on my thigh that says 'Drag Queen'. We don't care what you are. We don't care what kind of drag you do, but we do care about how you do it. It needs to be done well. That's all we care about – that you do it well. Are you versatile? Can you bring more than just the one thing to the party? Then *Drag Race* is for you!

And thankfully the UK queens have not let us down – in fact they have delivered more than I ever anticipated because they actually understand that their aesthetic is different to their sisters' in the States. Brit Queens are in a world of their own and that's what we wanted to highlight. We wanted to celebrate the gritty 'roughness' and 'ropiness' of the UK scene but we also wanted to see the heart of British drag. I don't care if you're from Scotland, Wales, England, whatever part of the country you're from, it's all about heart and that's the beauty of British drag and I'm so pleased we convey that on the show, and I hope the girls from all seasons are proud of who they are.

Now, my beautiful angels, it's time for me to sashay away and let you jump into the rest of this extravaganza eleganza of an annual and let you meet some old and new queens.

Have fun!

Welcome to

Ru's World

Start your engines!

Hello, hello, hello ...

Welcome to the first ever official *Drag Race* book! It's been a long time coming and we hope you love it.

But before you dive into this celebration of all things *Drag Race UK*, first a little history lesson...

A LITTLE HISTORY LESSON

It's hard to believe that it was way back in 2009 that *Drag Race* quietly launched on Logo TV, complete with the now-infamous season one filter.

While back then the show might not have boasted the plush sets and A-list celeb judges we are used to today, we worked out pretty fast that it not only entertained us, but pulled at our heart strings as the queens opened up about their lives.

Since then, we have laughed and cried and laughed again as talented queens from across the globe have sashayed into our lives, won our hearts and taken their rightful place in *Drag Race* history.

But long before *Drag Race* was even a sparkle in RuPaul's glitter-speckled mind, the sassy supermodel had already carved out a hugely successful global career.

GOING BACK TO RU'S ROOTS

From the day he was born in San Diego RuPaul had stars glimmering in his eyes. Even then his mum Ernestine Fontenette could see his sickening potential, and named him RuPaul Andre Charles because 'he is going to be a star and no other motherf****r would have a name like that'.

By the time he was 15, the ambitious young queen had headed to Atlanta with his sister Renetta to study performing arts. There he stunned his fellow students with his 'freaky' home-made clothes. But he loved being different and when at 16 he saw *The Rocky Horror Picture Show* for the first time, he found an inner confidence that led him to embrace being different and who he really was.

After college, Ru wanted to be a star and light up the sky with his name, just like his idol Irene Cara from *Fame*. So throughout the Eighties, Ru began to develop his drag persona and started to carve out a career as a musician and filmmaker, appearing on Atlanta's public-access variety show *The American Music Show*.

It was here in Atlanta that he met Fenton Bailey and Randy Barbato, who were in a band at the time called 'The Fabulous Pop Tarts'. They stumbled upon her dressed in thigh-high boots, a jockstrap and football shoulder pads, busy pasting pictures of himself on walls with the words 'RuPaul is EVERYTHING!' They knew straight away that Ru was destined for big things.

Under their guidance, Ru released a spin-off album from his now-legendary cult movie *Starrbooty*, which cost him just $100 to make, and copies of which were sold out of a shopping trolley. Not exactly a Hollywood fairy tale, but it certainly put Ru on the map!

SUPERMODEL OF THE WORLD

The unstoppable team continued to go from strength to strength in the nineties, with Fenton and Randy helping Ru to reinvent himself as a glamazon drag queen.

Not only did he release the iconic international hit 'Supermodel (You Better Work)' on rap label Tommy Boy, he also teamed up with MAC Cosmetics and became the first drag queen ever to be a spokesmodel for a cosmetics company. Ru also appeared on TV shows Manhattan Cable and Ring My Bell, which were produced by the mighty World of Wonder, the production company Fenton and Randy had set up.

It wasn't long before RuPaul was a global superstar, securing a regular spot on the UK's *This Morning* and even teaming up with Sir Elton John not only to host the BRIT Awards in 1994, but to release a disco cover of his old classic 'Don't Go Breaking My Heart'!

For the rest of the Nineties, Ru hosted a variety of TV shows, made cameo appearances in movies like *To Wong Foo, Thanks For Everything! Julie Newmar* and *The Brady Bunch Movie*, continued to release music and teamed up with MAC to become the first drag queen ever to be a spokesmodel for a cosmetics company.

RUPAUL'S DRAG WHAT?

Fifteen years later, *Drag Race* was born.

The idea of a TV show had been tossed about for years, but nobody could decide exactly what kind of vehicle they wanted to produce for Ru. Ru said he'd be up for anything as long as it wasn't an elimination competition show.

Eventually, however, he came to like the idea and after tossing some ideas around, they dreamt up the concept of *Drag Race* and began shopping it around the networks. Unfortunately, no one took the show seriously to begin with.

'The climate was different,' Fenton remembers. 'Nowadays, of course, it's a no-brainer – drag and TV go together like peanut butter and jelly. It seems hard to remember a time when drag queens weren't on TV. But there was such a time.'

And then, luckily for the world, Ru and his team came across a small channel called Logo, which specialised in LGBTQ+ programming.

With a minuscule budget to play with, Ru and World of Wonder produced the soft-filtered first season of *Drag Race* in a tiny studio in north Los Angeles, where the control room was no bigger than a broom closet. While it was a little rough around the edges, viewers bought into the show straight away and the rest, as they say, is history.

ALL HAIL THE UNITED QUEENDOM

Having grown up in the UK, Fenton always had it in mind to bring the show across the pond.

But once again he and his WOW team faced an uphill struggle. Although he knew a British audience would lap up the series, it was telly execs who were harder to convince, even though the show was an Emmy-winning global sensation.

'Almost from the beginning, I would go round pitching *Drag Race* to UK networks and I'd get asked, "What is *Drag Race*? Is it some kind of motorcar thing?"' Fenton recalls. 'What changed was, an executive at a network we spoke to about it for the umpteenth time said, "My kid loves that show!"'

With feverish expectation surrounding a British version of *Drag Race*, Ru and WOW knew they had to choose the best cast they could to launch the series in the UK. Luckily, they discovered that the UK was bursting with eager queens.

'From the moment Baga Chipz walked in talking about loving a battered sausage and being covered in Daddies Sauce, we knew it was going to be great!' Randy says.

Wow! Can we get an amen up in here!

Of course, as we all know, the iconic show is a huge success with spin-offs in the States such as *All Stars*, *Untucked!*, *Secret Celebrity Drag Race*, *Werq the World*, and *God Shave the Queens*. Today in addition to the little old UK, there are original versions of *Drag Race* all around the world – Chile, Thailand, Canada, Holland, Spain, Australia and New Zealand. There's also DragCon in Los Angeles, New York and London, a well as a live show in Las Vegas. This is just the tip of the iceberg.

The future looks even more spectacular!

You're a winner baby!

We may be excited about the crowning of DRUK's third Drag Superstar, but let's not forget the queens who triumphed before her – the mighty Lawrence Chaney and the dazzling Vivienne.

LAWRENCE CHANEY

The Drag Race *season two finale had fans around the world gagging.*

Condragulations on winning season two, Lawrence! Life must be a blur for you.

It's been busy! There's been a lot of work and a lot of pressure because for some reason I'm seen by some people as the be-all and end-all of British drag. Life has really changed. I've been doing interviews, TV shows and I've even been writing a book.

You've been a massive fan of *Drag Race* for years. What's the show meant to you?

It's the Holy Grail! It's really amazing. I grew up in rural Scotland where there are no drag queens. I mean, there'd probably be a local scandal if someone's husband wore a dress as a joke one night down the pub. It was that kind of place. There were really no drag artists, very few queer people, no PoC, nothing. So, when I saw the show for the first time, I was so utterly amazed by it – it was almost a culture shock.

What made it so iconic?

The show made me realise that I never knew so many people like me existed around the world. And it felt nice, because where I was in Scotland I was getting bullied for being who I was, for being different. I was getting bullied for having weird hair. But on *Drag Race*, RuPaul was making jokes about being gay and everyone was laughing and you could win a prize if you were crowned the next Drag Superstar. I knew as soon as I watched it, it would change my life.

Had you come out at this point?

No, I hadn't and I'd not really started drag either, though I'd started playing around with make-up, as one does. I was about 13, so very young. But I started getting more experimental with drag when I discovered that my mum loved RuPaul, knew 'Supermodel (You Better Work)' and was aware of legendary drag queen Divine. However, she wouldn't let me watch the movie *Pink Flamingos* [which Divine starred in] because she said it was too rude. But I guess she was only keeping an eye out for me.

So, how did you finally broach your interest in drag with your mum?

To start with I said to her that I wanted to dress up because I wanted to make people laugh, like Matt Lucas and David Walliams did and the old-school comedians like Stanley Baxter and Les Dawson she'd grown up with. What they did was basically drag too, whether they had covered eyebrows or not. So my mum let me play around with make-up, and I had fun. Then it developed into that kind of glamazon-inspired look with the eyebrows 'up here', and that's when I

decided to speak to my mum, as I didn't want her worrying about me when I went out to a show. At the same time I'd been talking to this guy and felt ready to come out. I thought it'd be fine because my mum's nice, but I just started crying, 'Mum, I'm gay!!!!!' It was just a big nightmare. And she took it amazingly.

She sounds like you – she loved RuPaul back in the day and she's obviously someone with an open mind.

Yes, absolutely, and I think I have Ru to thank for that, because my mum probably wouldn't be as accepting now if it wasn't for Ru coming out with [...] big hair and glamorous dresses in the eighties. So being on the show is like a full-circle moment.

So meeting Ru must have been everything to you!

I loved meeting her. She was really sweet. When Ru first said my name in the way she did I thought she was taking the piss. I thought, 'Does she hate me?' But as it evolved over the weeks she was really nice and we spoke a lot – we'd chat. It's lovely to watch back. Even in those bad episodes when I'm angry, there were nice moments in there between me and Ru!

Drag Race seems to be a beacon for young LGBTQ+ people who feel isolated. The show has helped make drag culture more mainstream.

It is much easier to be a queen these days, and thank God for it. There's make-up readily available in Boots that is better fitted for drag. I'm happy about the kind of exposure that drag now has thanks to the show. However, I do think some people take up drag to be famous. Well, that's not the reason why you do drag! You do drag because you love it and you love performing and sewing. That's why I did it. I loved sewing and making people laugh, so I just combined it all into one thing.

What advice have you got for future queens?

What you do is: you need to turn up to shows, meet people, talk, have a laugh with them, get drunk with them. It's all about the shared experiences. That night out is an investment. But some of them will say, 'Oh, well, I don't go anywhere when I'm not paid,' and I'm like, 'You're getting £15! Do you not want to talk to the bar owner and try to get £25 the next time and start building your way up?'

Looking back at your season, do you have any regrets?

The episode where I kicked off at Ellie about the comedy line-up was cringey. I'd just bombed another comedy challenge so I was super insecure about the placement Ellie was putting us in. I was worried that if I messed up again I would go home. I think if Tayce had thrown me under the bus like that I would've been like, 'Fair enough,' because I didn't know her. But because I had a good bond with Ellie, it was different and so I let rip. We are good now, but it was so awkward watching it back.

THE VIVIENNE

All hail the original UK queen!

How has winning the show changed your life?

Drag Race has opened so many doors for me – doors I didn't even know existed. Never mind doors – it blew off the doors, the gates, the cattle grid! The lot! It's phenomenal.

With your busy schedule, has The Vivienne taken over your real life? What do you and your hubby get up to when you're not The Vivienne?

Well … David and I love to travel, so any opportunity we get, we love to go to Florida. We're huge theme-park geeks and I love *Jurassic Park*, so it's just bliss!!!

What's the best thing that has come from appearing on the show?

When fans tell me that sharing my story of addiction saved their lives … Now try telling me, 'It's just a drag show.'

Based on your own experience, what five tips would you offer future drag superstars?

Have confidence, learn your craft, make Ru LAUGH. Don't be bad and NEVER leave without that crown!

Bring back my girls

A history

PART 1 – DRAG RACE UK *IS ANNOUNCED*

When word reached our shores that Drag Race was coming to Blighty, some fans wondered how it would compare to the sick US version – but they were in for a big surprise. Now, with three seasons of Drag Race UK already in the bag, Baga Chipz, Bimini Bon-Boulash, Blu Hydrangea, Cheryl Hole, Divina de Campo, Lawrence Chaney, Tia Kofi and Veronica Green return to the werk room to look back at how the show has enraptured the world.

> 🔍 How did you feel when you heard Drag Race UK was on the way?

BAGA:

I was really excited, but I'll be honest, none of us could be sure what it was going to be like. Because we loved the American version so much, we were worried that it might not be as good. But the very second I walked into that werk room I was like, oh ... it's gonna be exactly the same as the American one. And it really is exactly the same. In fact, I think the UK werk room is actually better!

BIMINI:

I remember having a conversation with a friend in The Glory [pub] about what it might be like and we were in two minds about whether we should do it or not. Should we go for it this time? Or wait and see how the first series looked? I decided straight away that I wasn't ready, but my mate was up for doing it. To be honest, I wasn't even sure if I was going to be ready for season two. I'd actually dreamt I was going to go on and do well in season three. I usually think I've got good intuition, but I guess I was a bit off on that occasion.

CHERYL:

We all approach things with caution, but in general I tend not to overthink situations or let other people's pressures or thoughts creep into my own or overwhelm me. But as much as there was a pressure for the UK version to live up to the standard of the US seasons, I thought it'd be fun to give it a go, go in and say, 'I'm just going to be me,' do what I do best and have fun. And that resonated the most. I didn't put a pressure on myself to live up to other people's expectations. I just focused on being me – and it worked!

LAWRENCE:

I was never worried about what the UK version was going to be like. I knew it was gonna be amazing and so I auditioned for the first series. I think what makes the American one so special is that the queens come from all over America and bring their own flavours. That's how we got all these amazing phrases like 'hunty ass' and 'slay' and all that verbiage. It's all because people have come from all over the US with their own ways of saying something. And we Brits are the same. So who knows, maybe one day 'hiya hen' or 'aboot' or 'shagpipes' will become a staple on *Drag Race* around the world? But what I think makes the UK so special is that we're a small island with such a diverse, rich community, which is why I knew it was going to be amazing.

TIA:

The thing that stands out most about *Drag Race* UK is its heart. It's not always about the most polished queen, or the most glam one. It's about the pure heart of the drag performer. Which is why Baga was such a stand-out. I think she must have spent 50 pence on all of her drag for the series – and still got change. But she was still incredible throughout the whole thing. And all these stories we heard – like the wig Baga wore for her final performance was one that Cheryl had left for her – it's stuff like that that shows everyone is like a family.

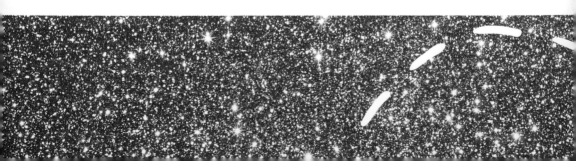

VERONICA:

I was super excited when I heard there was going to be a UK version. I had been waiting patiently for the show to come here and so I actually applied for the first series. In preparation, I taught myself to sew, as I knew that was a huge part of the show, and made my first outfit for my first audition tape. But I never heard back! I was gutted. I really wanted to be on the first season because I thought I was ready for it. But in hindsight, when I compare my two auditions tapes, I realise I was absolutely not ready for season one. I was only just starting to get to grips with who my persona was and how I performed in drag, so I'm glad I didn't get on the first season, because I would have been one of the first boots for sure.

DIVINA:

When I heard about the show, I had no hesitancy whatsoever, because I'd got to a stage in my life where I kept putting things off and thinking about doing them later. But then I came to realise that when opportunity knocks, you've got to take it and not worry about what will happen. Yes, there was an unlikely possibility the show could bomb, but would it damage your career beyond salvageability? *Drag Queens of London* [a schlocky 2014 reality TV series from yesteryear] had been terrible and everyone came out of that unscathed! Right, Baga? I was lucky to have had loads of opportunities in my life, so I saw *Drag Race* UK as the next practical step for me. I was thinking that if I do this, hopefully it will take me to the next level and open doors for me to be able to do things which I'd always wanted to do.

'I've never been so nervous to walk through a doorway in my life.'

Veronica Green

She's the comeback queen who needs no introduction. But we'll give her one anyway. Welcome back, Veronica Green, the musical-theatre queen.

Welcome back, Veronica. Being forced to pull out of season two because of COVID must have been totally devastating for you.

It was. When the show was halted it felt like my journey was over before I'd had a fair shot at it, and that was hard to deal with. Then, being asthmatic, I was worried about getting COVID. There were just so many different thoughts and feelings in my head and I was trying to pull myself through it and drag myself into a good headspace so that I could prepare myself to go back for the second half of the series. Then two days before filming was due to resume, I got a call. I'd tested positive for COVID, I couldn't go back. I was heartbroken. It was hard being at home, but thankfully, I recovered quite quickly. Plus, finding out that RuPaul had given me an open pass to return for another series made me feel a whole lot better! It's been a bit of a roller coaster ride and since the show went out, I've been overwhelmed by all the love from the fans, so I guess it all worked out in the end!

So was returning to series 3 a hard decision to make?

It was a no-brainer! The deciding factor for me was: I'd be the first ever queen to do two seasons in a single year and the first queen to ever go back with a challenge win under their belt, because no other returning queen has ever done that.

And you really excelled in *Rats: The Rusical*.

I did - Rat bite fever! I knew I just needed to nail the performance. I was very fortunate to have delivered both a great performance and a great runway. I felt I was 100 per cent a winner and I will cherish my Ru Peter badge forever - It's on my bedroom windowsill. I look at it every morning to get me out of bed!

The other queens said they looked up to you because you had been there before, were you less nervous second time round? Did it still feel like all your dreams came true?

Oh absolutely, it's been an amazing experience. I've never been so nervous to walk through a doorway in my life. You truly can't replicate it. Seeing RuPaul for the very first time was very surreal. You'd think going through the door a second time would feel the same, but it's not. It's completely different and I was just as nervous, if not more!

Did you find it easy to standout?

I think so. One thing you can't deny is that I've got a really great personality, I am quick witted and I do have a funny persona and my own signature style, which is something that nobody else has. So I do think that I am very unique and very individual. I have a lot of experience outside of drag as a performer and because entertaining has been my life since drama school. I trained to do this. This is in my blood. Although drag is something that's relatively new to me, it that just a part of being a performance artist.

'It was an amazing experience.'

Chose your Drag Name

Once you've worked out your drag persona and aesthetic, it's time to find that all-important name. This is probably the most important thing any queen can do. Why? Because not only does it tell your audience a little something about you, if catchy and memorable, it will stick in the minds of those who come to watch you throw shade.

But finding that special name isn't easy. Some can be based on the monikers the queens were actually born with, such as Joe Black and of course our own momma Ru herself. Others can be flamboyant and made up of a dazzling combination of sassy words and surnames that have a certain eleganza extravaganza – think Krystal Versace or Ellie Diamond. Some can be kooky like Bimini Bon Boulash and Baga Chipz, some are naughty like A'Whora and Scarlett Harlett, whilst others utilise clever word play like Scaredy Kat, Elektra Fence, Charity Kase, and Kitty Scott-Claus.

When it comes to drag, the world is your oyster.

Here are a few quick steps to help to choose the perfect name.

1. Play around with words. Dream up a punny name like Victoria Scone or Courtney Act, which are designed to sound like everyday items or phrases.

2. Dig deep. Some queens use moments from their past to help them find their name. Elektra Fence chose her name based on an experience she'd had of actually being electrocuted on a fence.

3. Go for glamour. Many queens are inspired by showbiz and fashion – so:

The Vivienne is named after her favourite designer Vivienne Westwood, with the "The" thrown in for added grandeur.

Vanity Milan chose her name because Milan always serves fashion – and her mum nicknamed her Vanity as she loved looking in the mirror!

Cheryl Hole was inspired by her love of Girls Aloud and the artist formerly known as Cheryl Cole.

Anubis chose her name as a reference to the Egyptian God of the afterlife, and to pay homage to her Egyptian father.

Veronica Green and **Blu Hydrangea** feel like Superheroes in drag, so why not have superhero name.

Joe Black and **Lawrence Chaney** wanted to retain a little bit of their real-life names, but they added surnames that was a nod to their love of silver screen glamour.

Tayce went down the Rockstar route and dispensed with a surname!

Sister Sister chose her name after her favourite TV show and of course as a tribute to women!

Kitty Scott-Claus loves her puns, and British drag, so she plumped for one of her favourite sayings that felt quintessentially English.

Astinna Mandela is of course an homage to her hero, but her first name is a cheeky play on her birth name, Aston!

Choriza May is not just a clever word play on a former Prime Minister's name Theresa May, but it also references her Spanish immigrant status post Brexit.

River Medway is proof that sometimes geography can provide you with a glamorous drag name. For River's case it was simple – she's from a small Kent town famous for the River Medway!

Still finding it hard to find your name? Then, why not give our Drag Queen Name generator a spin and try a one or two out for size . . .

First initial of your first name	First name of your surname
A – Celeste	A – Lily
B – Tyra	B – Lamour
C – Lotta	C – Fontaine
D – Belle	D – Versace
E – Yasmine	E – Galore
F – Kylie	F – Black
G – Donatella	G – Evangelista
H – Cindy	H – Ritz
I – Felicia	I – Campbell
J – Eva	J – Sauvage
K – London	K – Taylor
L – Ivana	L – Hayworth
M – Opal	M – Davenport
N – Tatjana	N – Harlow
O – Naomi	O – Rivers
P – Stella	P – Monroe
Q – Coco	Q – Carrington
R – Gemma	R – Hilton
S – Christy	S – Summer
T – Amber	T – Swanson
U – Angela	U – McQueen
V – Tiffany	V – Travel Lodge
W – Helena	W – Paige
X – Paris	X – From HR
Y – Beverley	Y – Royale
Z – Spring	Z – Foxx

Note: Of course, you don't have to stick to the first name you come up with. Elektra Fence was originally called Robyn Banks, but changed it when she felt she had outgrown her original nom-de-plume.

The Library is Open

Time to get shady, y'all?

In the great tradition of Paris Is Burning, bring out your library cards! Because reading is what?

But before you start throwing shade, let's remember some of our Brit queens', filthiest moments.

Divina: Baga Chipz! More like Baga Shite! She's like class in a glass without the glass or the class.

The Vivienne: Crystal. My darling. How aptly named. Just like crystals, you are lifeless, stiff and I can see right through you!

Sister Sister: Lawrence Chaney, I lie in bed at night and wonder how you're getting on – getting on the bed without breaking it!

Lawrence Chaney: Ellie Diamond, you are so stupid I heard you studied for your COVID test!

Shady, right? Those queens are mean and we love it.

So what are the rules?

Don't be cruel. Pick on something that your victim is happy to joke about, not something that will have them crying!

Pick on something personal to them and make it funny. 'Sister Sister, love the new gnashers. But should you be walking the catwalk or running the Grand National!'

Try a fake compliment. 'Oh Kitty girl. I've admired for years how brave you – it takes real courage to turn up here wearing that!'

And if you're on the receiving end of the shade, don't take it too seriously. It's all part of the game.

So, with no further a do, the library is open...

So, are you ready to read?

Then cut out these dis-respectacles (take care when using scissors) and read your friends to filth.

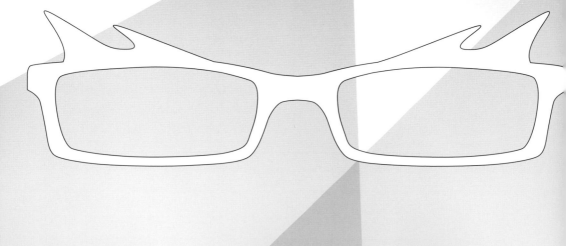

Decoration of your shady glasses is highly encouraged. Suggested additions: Environmentally friendly glitter, Feathers, Sequins, Paint, Rhinestones and Crystals!

Be kind. But be funny.

'I call myself
the Drag Beast
from the East.'

Ella Vaday

Please welcome Glamazon Essex queen Ella Vaday!

Welcome to the werk room. So you're season three's Essex queen!

I'm originally from Essex but grew up in the Suffolk countryside. So I'm very much east, so I call myself the Drag Beast from the East. I've been doing musical theatre for the last 13 years, covering lead roles in the West End and playing leads and I've been doing drag for the last two years properly.

How did you make the jump from the stage to drag?

My first time in drag was at a charity night called the MAD Drag Night, which is when all the West End performers pitch in to raise money. This was my first time dressing up in drag. I'd played around with wigs, just being silly, but never in a million years thought I could do drag. So this was like the perfect chance to get into make-up. Over time, my interest in the make-up and the creativity side of it really grew.

What was your first performance like?

When I first started, I was just working at a club night as a door host. Then I put myself out there, singing at different Prides. So then I launched my Ella Vaday Instagram in secret. I didn't even tell my best friends; I just put myself out there, because I was like, if I'm going to do this, I'm going to do it properly. So I did!

So what made you think you were ready for *Drag Race*?

I can sing. I can act. I am funny. I've got the looks. I can do the make-up. I've got the package. And after a year of lockdown I was like, why the hell not? I'm 32. If I don't do it now, I'll never do it.

How would you describe Ella's look?

It's kind of a heightened, feminine sort of portrayal. I think in my normal life I try to be very masculine, like a standard guy. Especially with my job, I've always tried to be more muscular and handsome and what you think of as a leading male. So my drag is absolutely the opposite. She's curvy, she's got a tiny waist, she's got tits and all this hair. I see her like a Jessica Rabbit-kind of woman. She's so fake it's clear I'm not really a woman, but women are like, 'Oh my God, you're gorgeous.'

What was it like stepping into the werk room for the first time?

It was like stepping into the TV. I felt like I wasn't even there – it was like an out-of-body experience, like stepping in and saying a line to the cameras. It was like, 'Oh my God, I can't believe I am actually here.' I didn't expect the whole set to be 360. I just thought one side would be completely blank. You walk in and you're like, 'This is what I see on telly. This is weird. And why am I here? What am I doing here?' It's so weird. But it was very exciting and very surreal.

Being older than the other contestants, do you think you brought wisdom to the younger queens?

I grew up in the early nineties and, for me, growing up gay was like a big sin and it was a horrible thing to be. And so I avoided it for most of my life. I tried my hardest not to be gay! When I was growing up my mum and dad were arguing a lot and they got divorced and I was the older kid who was looking after everyone. So the last thing I even thought about was my sexuality. I kind of pushed that to the side and that's basically what I did most of my life – just avoided thinking about it and pretended. It was like, 'Oh no, I just want to look like everybody else.'

So when did you finally come out?

I didn't come out until I was about 21 or 22, which is surprising when you've been at a musical-theatre college since 16. I told all of my family differently. I told my brother first – who's straight and went to drama school – who said, 'Is this the bit when you tell me you're gay?' Then I had to get really drunk to tell my mum. It was all good. There were no issues. You always think it's going to be a huge issue, but then it's really not.

Who were your initial favourites on season two?

I felt Lawrence really stood out from the get-go. When they all came back after the COVID break, it shifted. I feel like Lawrence had gone in as the clear frontrunner. Then the gap happened and people came back and they were like, 'Right, we're gonna take this.' It felt like Bimini had stepped up the game and Tayce did too. A'Whora went from the villain at the beginning and then turned into this really nice person. I've met her as well and she's so nice.

'I can sing. I can
act. I am funny.
I've got the looks.
I can do the
make-up. I've got
the package.'

Super Heroes Assemble

Drag Origins

Every queen has to start somewhere …

DragRaceUK

CHERYL HOLE: 'Drag Race helped me pass my degree!'

I was studying contemporary dance at university at the time and I was really struggling with what I wanted to do. All I knew was, I wanted to dance and perform and be fabulous. So I started breaking all the norms of what my lecturers wanted, embraced the idea of what contemporary means and started doing my own thing. I got lower grades, I admit, but in the grand scheme of things it helped me grow as an artist. *Drag Race* really influenced my work towards the end of my degree and I left with a 2:1 and decided, 'I am going to do drag.' Then I started doing a few gigs and got into a competition in London and then my drag career kickstarted from there!

DIVINA DE CAMPO: 'I was living on £15 a week until I became a drag queen!'

I came to drag from a more academic route. I'd been reading loads of gender-politics, gender-equality stuff at university and then went off to work as a dancer, not earning much money. Then my husband-to-be, who ran nightclubs, suggested I try drag, telling me I could earn £150 a night if I was good! At this point I was living off £15 a week after bills.

It took me probably five years to settle on the name Divina de Campo. At first I ran a 'Name the Queen' competition and got loads of horrendous names. I reminded myself, your name is your calling card, it has to make sense and give the audience a flavour of what you're about. I was singing Italian opera and people would say, 'Ain't she campo?' all the time. Then I saw this drag queen called Divina Ponds and I thought that sounded Italian. Divina means 'divine',and campo means 'a

DragRaceUK

field', which is the first place I had sex, so for me that all kind of made sense. And Divina de Campo was born.

LAWRENCE CHANEY: 'I was inspired by an old Hollywood horror actor!'

I became inspired by the 1920s Hollywood actor Lon Chaney, who was in classic horror films like *The Phantom of the Opera* [1925], *The Hunchback of Notre Dame* [1923], *London After Midnight* [1927]. He inspired me because he was an actor who did his own make-up, did everything himself, and he made it gruesome and spectacular.

A'WHORA: 'I did drag as a revenge thing!'

When I was younger I was in a bad relationship with a guy who would constantly tell me I wasn't masculine enough for him. I lost all my personality. I never laughed. I became obsessed with my image so that I looked the way he wanted me to look. Then one day he told me he didn't want to be with me. That's when the seed for A'Whora was planted. He'd always told me I was too femme for him, so I thought to myself, 'How can I be the most feminine version of myself' So I decided to do drag.

BIMINI BON-BOULASH: 'I did a year of sobriety with no alcohol, no drugs!'

When I was in my teens I went through more image changes than Madonna. I was always reinventing myself. When I first moved to London, I got caught up in the hedonism of it and started hanging out with loads of queens. They were people that I thought were incredible and had so much confidence – something I was lacking at the time. In 2019, I won the Miss Sink The Pink competition and people saw I was one to watch and then I just grafted for that year. I started taking it a bit more seriously and did a year of sobriety with no alcohol, no drugs, which was hard when you're working on the scene. I did it for a year and then I applied for *Drag Race* and got on and was like, 'Well, I better get ready.'

BAGA CHIPZ: 'A drunken night as Amy Winehouse kicked off my drag career!'

My mate Raven was always going on about me dressing up as a girl. One night we went out to a karaoke night we went to every week in Birmingham – dressed as a draggy Amy Winehouse. When the bar host, Mrs Moore, clapped eyes on me in my Amy get-up she said, 'Get up here and sing us a song.' And so I did. Before I could get myself another drink, the owner of the bar came up to me and told me he thought I'd done a brilliant job and said that if I sang more songs like that for the rest of the evening, he'd give me free drinks. I mean, it was already a quid a drink all night, but what kind of bloody idiot would I be to turn down the offer of free booze, eh?

At the end of the night, the big boss of the club pulled me to one side and said to me, 'Can you do what you did tonight every Friday for £100?' Without pausing for breath, I bit his hand off before he could change his mind.

'There's nothing worse than when you need a wee and your knob's between your legs.'

Elektra Fence

Please welcome the beauty from Burnley, Elektra Fence!

Condragulations on making it into season three of *Drag Race UK*. You've come a long way from Burnley!

I have. And I am so excited to be part of the show. It's like a dream come true.

What was walking into the werk room like?

It was weird. I was stood there in the wings, thinking I was going to walk out there and everyone was going to say, 'You've been Punk'd!' So when I did walk in all I could hear was the clip-clop of my heels. I heard the girls and they were like, 'Woooo!' Then I heard Vanity say, 'Oh God, you don't want to lip sync against her, I know what she can do.' And I was like, 'Yeah, you better be scared!' It felt great because I was like, 'Oh my God, they know me.' And then I turned around and saw some of my friends, like Kitty and Vanity.

A lot of this year's cast are musical-theatre queens, aren't they?

They are, which I saw as an advantage, cos I can sing. Well, I can hold a tune, but I'm not Ella Vaday or Kitty, who love to sing. I dance. We all have things we bring to the stage. No one's shy in our cast!

And Victoria Scone is bringing something very different to the stage as well.

Yes, she has an amazing breast plate. I'm not sure where she got that from!

What was it like meeting Ru for the first time?

It was incredible. You hear the door go and you're like, 'Oh, that's RuPaul behind you.' And I needed a wee so bad and my feet were killing me. There's nothing worse than when you need a wee and your knob's between your legs. It was just incredible and amazing.

The werk room must be a lot different to growing up in Burnley.

Let's just say my town was not very progressive back in the day. It's more gay-friendly now, but it wasn't when I was growing up. It wasn't very hip and happening. That's mainly why I ended up moving to London. Burnley's good for a night out. The football team are really good as well, but that's about it, really. There is one gay bar called Garden Bar, but when I was a kid growing up, people would say to me to never go in there. Obviously now I know it was a gay bar. It's funny to think there was just one gay bar in Burnley and there was one gay there as well – me! Ha!

Burnley is near Blackpool – did you enjoy the scene there?

I went to college in Blackpool – it's like a drag queen's handbag spilled everywhere; it's camp as tits. I am always shocked when I hear people say they haven't been to Blackpool. Even my partner has never been. I'm like, 'How come?' Go in the summer, though. In the winter you see it for what it is. But when the lights are on it's a lot better.

How did you deal with the bullying?

Well, some of the things that the boys used to say were about my parents, because both my parents are disabled. They have cerebral palsy. I was a young carer as well. Me and my brother, before he sadly passed away, were looking after my mum and my dad, but don't get me wrong – they looked after us and gave us the best life they could. We'd do things that normal children of that age wouldn't do – like I helped my mum walk upstairs, helped my mum make dinner and stuff like that. But I had the best childhood outside of school.

Did you feel like you grew up quickly?

Yeah, I did grow up very fast, especially when my brother died when I was 11. My parents were so distraught about my brother, and because it was just me I had more things to do. I want them to be proud, and want them to be proud of me on the show, because it is going to be epic.

How did you tell your parents you were gay?

I was always a bit different when I was younger. I didn't know what it was. I've always known there was something different, but I didn't actually come out until my 21st birthday. I was having a party with my mates and my mum said to me, 'Which one's your girlfriend?' I was pissed as a fart and said: 'Oh, Mum, none of these are my girlfriend.' And she went, 'Oh fine. We've always known.' I mean, looking back, they called me Julian! That's the campest name under the sun and I was doing ballet and tap and everything!

When was Elektra born?

Elektra was only born last year, but I had been doing drag for a while under the name Robyn Banks. Back in 2012, there was a viral video of me touching an electric fence and getting electrocuted by accident, which had over one million views on YouTube, so I changed my name to Elektra Fence.

When did you see *Drag Race* for the first time?

I saw *Drag Race* back in 2014, so that's one of the main reasons why I started drag. It was the series with Sharon Needles and my fascination just started from there.

So when the first series came on, did you think the Brits were as good as the Americans?

I knew this was going to be a good show. The moment Baga walked in, I was like, oh God, this is proper good telly – the kind of telly you sit down with a nice cuppa tea and pie and gravy to watch.

'It was incredible. You hear the door go and you're like, "Oh, that's RuPaul behind you".'

Not a Joke. Just a Fact.

The world according to Bimini Bon-Boulash, superstar!

The mighty Lawrence Chaney may have been crowned the UK's next Drag Superstar, but fellow finalist Bimini Bon-Boulash has discovered – like Baga before her – that being runner-up doesn't stop you from becoming a sickening success.

Since season two ended, the East-London queen has gone from strength to strength and has been splashed across glossy mags like Vogue and Dazed.

Here, the fabulous fashionista rummages around in our drag bag of random questions and shares some fascinating insights into her life and the world around her!

What three things do you carry with you at all times?

My phone, my lip gloss and my Monzo card – how boring, right?

Why is East London your favourite place to live?

Because the queer scenes in East London are what raised me as a queer person. And it's always been about having fun over anything else.

Linda Evangelista once said she'd only get out of bed for £10,000. How much would it take for you?

I'd get out of bed for an Uber and a sparkling water.

If you ran the world, what law would you create?

I would dismantle the patriarchy and have queers, females, a diverse range of people run the world, rather than the demographic that has done it for so many years. I genuinely think that if a woman politician led every single country in the world, we would never have a war. I think men are too aggressive to run countries.

Is there a high-street store you wouldn't step into?

All of them. I get [clothes] online, or from second-hand places or Depop.

If you released a perfume, what would it smell like?

It would have hints of oat. It would have hints of depression and it would have hints of ... no, it wouldn't. It would smell lush! I'm just thinking about when I was a horny teenager.

What is it about the nineties that you love so much?

People seemed to let loose a bit more. There was no social media back then, so there were none of these avenues where you're comparing yourself to other people, apart from in magazines. I feel sorry for my little sister, who's completely missed out. Everything's so instant on her phone that no one wants to buy a glossy mag anymore. I felt like the nineties was really coming into its own. There were young, budding designers in the UK, like McQueen and Galliano, and they were always coming up with fresh ideas and wanting to do new things. It was just so interesting.

If someone says or does something bad, should they be history?

I don't believe in the whole cancelling thing. Look at people like Kate Moss, who I absolutely adore, who got destroyed in the media years ago because of that cocaine scandal. She was completely cancelled, but then came back. I think people deserve second chances; people deserve forgiveness. I think cancelling anyone is just reductive. We should be focusing on people who are doing really bad things, not celebrities who put their foot out of place.

What's your secret talent?

I did it in the last episode of *DRUK* – the Russian can-can.

Prince Harry or Prince William?

Prince Harry, because I love Princess Diana – she was a rebel. I got into Diana's story quite late. But I really love her and I think she used fashion as a tool. I mean, that infamous revenge dress she wore back in the day. Iconic!

What nineties fashion look would you bring back?

Pencil-thin eyebrows – it's what I've been trying to do.

How many pairs of shoes do you have?

I have a lot of shoes. My most precious pair are my ten-inch-high black pleasers and also my Vivienne Westwood schoolgirl shoes.

What's your earliest memory?

My earliest memory is scraping off the turquoise-blue paint off my auntie's car with a stone so that me and my cousin could paint on the floor. She wasn't happy!

Best rumour you've heard about yourself?

That I'm six foot four when I'm only five foot six and a half. The same size as Kate Moss.

What is your ultimate dream?

My ultimate life dream is to work towards changing people's minds and perceptions on sexuality, gender – and just really working towards more acceptance for everyone. And for people to know that the common enemy that we are all trying to fight is the patriarchy.

Instagram.com/biminibabes

'We all had our
own experiences,
which makes life
in the werk room
so interesting.'

Meet the Queens confessionals

Kitty Scott-Claus

Meet the hilarious Kitty Scott-Claus – a Brummy, London-based musical-theatre queen.

Condragulations, Miss Kitty, on becoming a season three queen!

Hoorah! I know, can you believe it? I still can't! It's like I'm appearing on my favourite show in the world. It's just unbelievable.

So, we take it you've been a fan of the series for years then?

I remember playing one of the ugly sisters in *Cinderella* at the time and I didn't really have any idea of how to do the make-up. Then a friend asked me if I had seen *Drag Race* and I was like, 'No!' I'd heard of it, but I'd never sat down and watched it. So I went round to his house with a group of mates and watched it.

And you liked it?

I was absolutely gobsmacked. They weren't what I thought drag queens were. I had grown up with pantomime dames and UK drag, which in my head was a Blackpool queen singing and shouting abuse at people. So to see these beautiful creatures on the TV was just amazing. I fell completely and madly in love with it. And then when the opportunity arose for me to actually do drag, I was like, 'Yes, I will. Yes, I bloody will.'

When did you swap pantos for drag queens?

My best friend was a drag queen and she used to work at a bar in Camden called Her Upstairs, which decided to put on a Girls Aloud night. And they said to me, 'We need a Kimberley Walsh.' I was like, 'I could do that,' even though I'd never done drag before in my life. But I had been an ugly sister, so I had that experience. So it started off doing a one-off gig at Her Upstairs in Camden, and then it just snowballed from there and Kitty was born!

So what had you been doing prior to this?

I'd been studying musical theatre. That's my background. I went to Mountview drama school in North London for three years.

So how has Kitty developed over the years?

There's not really any difference between when I'm out of drag and when I'm in drag. I went through a couple of drag names before I chose Kitty Scott-Claus. In the early days I thought I'd be Madonna Kebab or Chelsea Bun. It was only when I said something rude to my friend and they said, 'Oooh, saucer of milk?' that I said, 'Kitty's got claws.' As soon as I heard it out loud, I decided, 'That's my drag name.' So when the opportunity arrived, that became Kitty Scott-Claus. And the look? Well, I grew up with Barbies and Bratz dolls, so the vision of beauty for me was big blonde hair, big bust, hyper-feminine – not a very progressive look. To me, though, that is my vision of beauty. Because I'm blonde, I'm also looking at women who really inspire me like my mum, my sister, my aunties – they're all big, blonde women. I'm like, that's who Kitty is.

What was Kitty Scott-Claus like when he was 12?

When I was at school, I was quite cheeky. I learned very quickly, if you're funny, you can get away with a lot. So I used to do impressions of all the teachers, but to their faces. I would literally mimic them. I love impressions. It's my sense of humour to a T. The teachers found it funny, but now, looking back, I was a cocky little kid. I never got in trouble. I was always good as gold, but I had an edge. And that edge was being GAAAAY! I never had to come out – it really was a shock for no one.

Which of the season one queens were your favourites?

My standout star has got to be my sister Cheryl Hole. She was there for my first drag gig and I love her to the ends of the earth. I bloody love her. I thought she was brilliant. I also loved Baga, but I just find Baga so funny. I do a Spice Girls show as well – I was Ginger Spice and Baga was Mel C. Baga's Snatch Game was so good. That was like such a standout for me. It's always the Snatch Game for me because I just find it so funny.

When you walked into the werk room for the first time, did you know any of the other queens?

I was so excited walking in, thinking that this is my moment, to quote Martine McCutcheon. Move over, Martine, this is MY moment! When I went in I knew most of the girls on my season, but then I'm a social Sally, so don't begrudge me for being popular!

'When the opportunity arose for me to actually do drag, I was like, "Yes, I will. Yes, I bloody will".'

The Drag Race UK Hall of Fame

Which of the queens had charisma, uniqueness, nerve and talent?

Our sequin-spangled panel – A'Whora, Baga Chipz, Blu Hydrangea, Cheryl Hole, Divina de Campo and Tia Kofi – reveal their nominees.

The category is ...
THE QUEEN OF CHARISMA

Which of the girls had that certain something that kept their fellow queens gagged ...?

DIVINA: Oh my God, it has to be Baga Chipz. She's just so lovable, in't she? Even that week when she was really struggling with her mum and we saw a very different side to her, she was still so lovable. It never mattered what she looked like, because we were always going to like her.

CHERYL: Oh darlin', I think Baga had great charisma. There's just something about her that is hilarious. You can't help but watch her when she's onstage. But, for me, Tayce wins hands down for the second season. Her confessionals were just brilliant!

BLU: Baga had all the charisma in the world – you had to love her even though she drew horrible eyebrows on her mum and said she was too fat to fit into sexy dresses. But at the end of the day you're like, 'That's Baga Chipz.' I love her! For season two, I think Tayce was very charismatic. Beans on toast was already a tradition across the UK, but even more so now because of Tayce.

A'WHORA: For me, it has to be Baga Chipz and Tia Kofi. They were the ones with shedloads of charisma! They have a likeability factor and they're naturally welcoming people and are the kind of queens that if they're on a stage, they would just entertain you by talking. They are more relatable because they're not the most glamorous of drag queens. They feel like they could be your friend. Their character just entices you in and you want to hang out with them!

TIA: I have to say Baga for season one – you can't take your eyes off her because she is so funny. And for the sake of my own confidence, I'd say me for season two as no one else will ever say that!

BAGA: Why, me, of course! I think I was the funniest. I think my confessionals were funniest without a bloody doubt. I had wit. I had fierce comebacks. It does help if you've got stage experience. If you work on stages in pubs and someone's heckling yer it's good to have an answer for everything, and it's good to have a funny answer, not just, 'Oh, well, you're ugly.' It's gotta be like, 'If you don't like it, there's a bloody Wetherspoon's up the road.' Know what I mean?

SERIES 1 WINNER

SERIES 2 WINNER

The category is …
THE QUEEN OF UNIQUENESS

Which of the queens immediately stood out?

BLU: Am I allowed to say myself? I was pretty unique, as I was the only one from my series who could do their own make-up! But if I had to say someone else I would say Crystal, who was the most underrated unique queen of my season. She was just fabulous. She was quieter than the rest of us, but I think she's just amazing. You never knew what she was gonna do and also she's very handsome! For season two, I'd choose Cherry Valentine. Unfortunately, we never got to see too much of her, but that's just the way the cookie crumbles. But from what we did see I think she was very unique. She had this alien look about her that set her out from the rest.

TIA: For season one, I'd say Crystal was the most unique with her angle grinder and whips on the runway! Poor Geri Horner didn't know what to think or where to look! Bless her. And in my season, well, I have to say Bimini has a uniqueness that really stands out. I'd also suggest that Sister Sister had what you might call uniqueness, as nobody else

would dare put those patterns together like she did – and she was very confident in doing so.

BAGA: I'd say bloody me again. That's why I did so well on the show and outside of it. People are like, 'Oh, she's mental.' 'Oh, she's loud.' 'Oh, we've never seen anything like Baga apart from … well, Lily Savage.' But I've never seen a drag queen like me. My choice for season two is Bimini. She is quite unique. We've seen fashion queens before, but she took it to a new level. She might be vegan, non-binary and very PC, but she can also take the piss out of herself.

A'WHORA: I'd say for season one, Blu Hydrangea because of the way she incorporates her make-up into the actual aesthetic of her clothing. If there's a print in her outfit, she'll put that print into her make-up. Whereas if I had a blue dress, I'd just do a blue eyeshadow. I keep it simple. In season two I'd choose Cherry Valentine, as she has a really unique approach to drag. If anyone's going to sit there and stone an Easter basket, and then stone 5,000 crystals to your face, you've got patience, girl. I ain't got the time for that.

SERIES 1 WINNERS

SERIES 2 WINNER

CHERYL: For me, Blu was the most unique queen of season one. Everything she did was amazing. She was a creation goddess. For the second season, I'd say Cherry Valentine, as she had looks that pushed the envelope. I wish we had got to see more.

The category is …
QUEEN OF NERVE

Which of the ladies had the cheek, the gall, the audacity, the gumption to make their indelible mark on their *Drag Race* squirrel friends?

DIVINA: From season one I'm going to say Scaredy Kat, just because she was seven months fresh out of the box and she had the absolute nerve to apply for the biggest drag show in the entire world. But good on her! I think if she'd stayed a bit longer we would have seen a much more interesting artist. There's a lot going on inside that head of hers.

BLU: Oooooh, I think probably Vivienne. She was strong all the way through the competition and did not show fear once, which the rest of us took as this cut-throat demeanour. In retrospect I think it's what you need to get to the final. You need that power, that strength and that something to propel you through the competition. I think she had that more than anyone else. In season two, Tia Kofi had a lot of nerve for wearing the most ugly outfits ever seen on *Drag Race* but wearing them so confidently. After the break she even had the cheek to say, 'I've worked on these outfits!' Er, how!?

CHERYL: In season one – I'm going to put it out there – I think I had a lot of nerve. I'd do anything! For season two, I reckon Joe Black had the absolute nerve for serving H & bloody M realness to Ru on the runway!

BAGA: Vinegar Strokes for her runways. I mean, Jesus!! You've got to have some bloody nerve to wear some of that! Oh and Divina, cos she would just call people out.

TIA: For the first season, I'd say Scaredy Kat, because she was 19, had never seen a drag show and she hadn't done anything outside of her bedroom. Also, her final line after her elimination was quite something – it really takes nerve to walk to the back of the runway when you're in a room full of seasoned queens and say, 'Not bad for a first gig!' and then walk off. What an icon! For season two, I'm gonna shout out Asttina Mandella. It took a lot of nerve, poise and confidence to be that kind of shining star when she was eliminated from the show in what she must have thought was a totally unexpected moment, by me of all people. I think she is so gorgeous and carries herself so well and has all the skill and all the talent – but never get bogged down in the drama and the arguments.

DIVINA: In season two I thought Tia had a lot of nerve, because she was just going, 'Yeah, whatever, fine, whatever, all right, guys.' She just didn't let anything faze her, whereas I'd have been a broken ball on the floor if I was getting her critiques. I'd have been crying my eyes out every five seconds.

A'WHORA: I'd probably say Vinegar Strokes from season one. I can't believe she had the gall to wear any of those outfits onstage. They were disgusting. Coming out looking like that and branding herself 'hodgepodge' – I mean, darling, that does take nerve. From my season, it has to be Joe Black for daring to wear that H&M dress. It was just unforgivable. But maybe I should be more positive and say Bimini, for having the nerve to be confident to go onstage and wear those ridiculous high heels with next to nothing on. She's got nerve, she's got confidence, she's got bloody balls.

SERIES 1 WINNER

SERIES 2 WINNER

The category is ... QUEEN OF TALENT

Which queen had it all and made sure everybody else mutha-tucking knew about it?

A'WHORA: In season one, I'd say Divina de Campo had the most talent. She can really entertain a group. She's got presence. She can actually dance, she can do the splits – which is good for a girl of her age. From season two, I'd say A'Whora – I hear she's very talented. Seriously, I'd say Bimini, because she's literally an all-rounder. I mean, the talent to get four badges is very impressive. And her chair work is impeccable.

BLU: If I don't say Divina I think she'd punch me in the throat. I mean, the girl can sing in eight different languages in five different octaves, while doing the splits. She can dance, she's a magician, an actor, a model. She's done everything and will tell you 20 times a day that she can do it all. I actually do believe she is very talented, as in the Frock Destroyers she's the only one of us who can hold a note, so it's great. The season two queens were all talented, but I'd have to choose Joe Black. She may have been eliminated first, but she's a great cabaret performer. Her old-school cabaret shows take you back to a thirties German bar, which is really camp. I knew of Joe prior to the show and I honestly said to him before he went in, 'You're going to make it to the end. There's no way in the world that you won't!' Then I got a message a few days later saying, 'Oh well, that didn't happen.'

BAGA: I thought Crystal was extremely talented when it came to sewing and making her dresses – they were beautiful. The Vivienne is like an all-rounder. She is funny, she can sing, she can lip sync, she can act, she can do stand-up comedy, she can make dresses, she can do her own wigs, her make-up is impeccable – she's a full package, she can do everything. She may not be able to do the splits and all that, but she can ... do the rest of it! Yeah, even more than me!

CHERYL: In the first season, we were spoilt for choice, but Divina and The Viv, they just had so much to offer – singing, dancing, comedy, acting; they did it all. In season two I reckon Lawrence and Bimini had the most talent, but in different ways. Lawrence was hilarious and had some great looks, and Bimini ... well, she was an amazing dancer and really pulled off some amazing looks in the later part of the series.

TIA: I think everyone in season one was talented in their own way, but to answer your question ... singing in five and a half octaves, it has to be Divina De Campo. Pure talent right there. From my season, I would say Tayce. That finale dance-number challenge – I was like, 'Did Tayce win the series?'

SERIES 1 WINNER

SERIES 2 WINNER

Drag Race

Drag can make your world a better place!

Saved
My Life

Drag is more than just dressing up, it's an art form. And for many queens it's armour: Sometimes, losing yourself in another persona can help you through the toughest of times. Here, Drag Race UK queens look back at how finding drag helped them survive.

ANUBIS: 'Without drag I really don't think I'd be here today ...'

I genuinely think I found my confidence through drag. art, music and songwriting. It was that release that took me out of a world that I wasn't enjoying very much. I was being verbally and physically abused at school. I was always good with a one-liner, but I think that made the bullies target me even more! I think they saw it as a bit of a challenge. You know, 'Let's pick on the gay fat kid.' If I didn't have things like music and drag, I really don't think I'd be here today, the creative outlet of performance really helped to get me through the low times. Now my drag makes me feel bulletproof.

VANITY MILAN: 'Drag gives you a different persona.'

When you put on make-up it changes the look, it changes the face. It definitely gives you a different persona and it definitely has got me through some tough times in my life. When you put the make-up on, you're like, 'You're beautiful.' Whereas as a boy sometimes I don't feel beautiful. If it gives somebody else confidence to see somebody like myself on television, I'm more than happy.

CHARITY KASE: 'Drag was a form of escapism for me.'

I started doing drag to help me through some dark periods in my life, as a form of expression. So it was a way of me getting my emotions out of my body and onto a canvas, which happens to be my face. So I'd paint sad characters if I felt sad, or angry characters if I felt angry. It was a form of escapism for me. It excited me to look in the mirror and not recognise myself at all.

CHERYL HOLE: 'Drag gives you that heightened moment!'

I always say the difference between me and Cheryl is an IV of Red Bull and 20 per cent more energy. That's all it is. If I can throw on a fabulous eye look, gorgeous hair and a shimmery rhinestone outfit, all I need is a trap door and a wind machine and I'm ready to go.

BAGA CHIPZ: 'Drag is basically a superhero costume!'

Drag transforms you! I would never act the way I do out of drag! It's basically a superhero costume. I put on the drag, the wig, and then you're like, 'Ooh, I'm ready to take on the world. I'm ready to become Baga Chipz and Baga Chipz takes no crap.' I've had times minding my own business when a bunch of straight blokes have walked past on a stag night and said, 'Ooh, is that a bloke?' and I'll tell them to get stuffed.' And they'd run off.' I'd never be that cocky out of drag!

TIA KOFI: 'To have that drag persona and to work in the bars that I do feels like home.'

I've always had the ability to brush things off, because life hasn't been an easy ride, regardless of whether I'm in drag or not. Being raised in suburban Essex in the nineties, I have always been a lanky, tall, skinny, six-foot-five brown boy with big, curly hair in a world where I stand out. It wasn't new for me to walk in and hear, 'Basic, basic, basic, basic,' and try to brush it off. I've had harsher words thrown at me for much of my life – it is what it is. To have that drag persona and to work in the bars that I do feels like home. As a queen, you are the focal point, so it's all about being warm, welcoming and encouraging, and also you get lots of free gin and tonics.

Bring back my girls

A history

PART 2 — SEASON TWO: A TOUGH ACT TO FOLLOW

A'Whora, Baga Chipz, Bimini Bon-Boulash, Blu Hydrangea, Cheryl Hole, Divina de Campo, Tia Kofi and Veronica Green continue to reflect on the second season of the global phenomenon ...

Even before the first season of Drag Race UK had finished its run, a second season was announced. Due to air around the autumn of 2020, casting began straight away and filming finally commenced in March 2020. The series eventually hit screens in January 2021, and proved to be an even bigger hit.

THE CLASS OF 2021

Season one had turned ten little-known queens into superstars. But were they ready to give up their crowns to a new batch of hungry girls?

When the new season aired, did you think, 'Oh God, there's a whole new set of queens about to be unleashed?'

DIVINA: In this kind of industry there's always that sort of fear that you'll be yesterday's news. But the only way to combat that is to get off your arse and go and do stuff. I've always been really proactive and productive, so I didn't really have that fear that suddenly everybody was going to leave my Instagram.

CHERYL: Nobody can steal my crown, darling. I am the queen of Essex. Nobody can take that from me. I saw so many kids online who'd say, 'If I was on the show, I would do this differently.' Well, it's one thing saying it, my loves, and one thing doing it. So I was so excited to sit back and go, 'Come on, kids, you see how hard it is. It's not easy.'

SEASON TWO AIRS

In January 2021, the second season launched during lockdown and the queens and the show became an instant hit.

Watching the season back, what did you make of the show?

TIA: It was incredible to watch. It was quite the season. It was a real rollercoaster ride for the viewers. The gag-worthy moments were aplenty – here, there and everywhere. As a viewer, I was still shocked that I stayed in over Asttina after that lip sync. We also had the first ever Rusical in the UK, which is a staple of *Drag Race*, and I still found it an honour to be chosen to cast it, despite being voted most basic queen by the girls.

THE EXPERIENCE

Drag Race may look like fun, but the queens of season two soon discovered how hard they have to work.

BIMINI: I would say in the first four episodes, I felt like I was having an out of-body experience the whole time. I was dead nervous. Being in the bottom in the first episode threw me off my game. No one expects it. I was like, 'I know what I'm capable of doing, but these people are not seeing it right away.'

TIA: Watching it back, I realised for the first time that Ru was fully in my corner, which was a proper gag. When you are there in the moment on the stage you are taking in your critique, but all I was hearing was, 'You're not doing it right.' Then I watched it back and I realised that wasn't what Ru was saying. She was actually telling me: 'If you do this, it will take you to the next level.' It was just amazing to gain that new perspective that Ru was on my side.

A'WHORA: It's weird watching yourself back and seeing yourself upset or in your proudest moments. I think the hardest part was watching my elimination week, because the week prior I'd experienced my highest high on the show. And then the following week I had my lowest low. It was such a flip of the script for me. It felt a bit cut-throat to relive it. But it's so good to watch the show from start to end, because you see two versions of yourself throughout one season.

Did you see the change in you?

A'WHORA: To see yourself grow over the space of a year and see it documented was insane. I cringed so much at myself. But then I was also happy, because I feel like I had one of the strongest arcs. You know, seeing someone come in with such a front and a hard face and trying to be something that I wasn't and prove a point, that I was valid, but fitting this *Drag Race* mould and then creating my own mould, and being my own artist – that's what was so cool, to see my whole character changed.

STAND-OUT STARS

With all the queens fighting for airtime and Ru's attention, some of the girls made their mark and caught the eye of the viewers.

Who caught your eye?

BLU: Lawrence was just fantastic and hilarious, and even when she had her stroppy diva moments – no one understands being in that werk room more than us queens. I've been in that situation, throwing wire hangers at people across the room!

DIVINA: My highlight was Bimini just full stop. The judges kept talking about her being scrappy and 'we can see your tape blah-blah-blah', but that's East-London drag, that's what it's supposed to be!

BAGA: I thought Tia Kofi showed a human side. She was relatable to the viewer. Us humans are not perfect, and Tia showed that. Not to sound shady, but she'd come out as a dog's dinner sometimes, but she was underestimated all the while, and when you get people talking and saying, 'This queen's bad,' it makes THEM look bad.

DRAMARAMA!

Season two served up its fair share of dramas during its run, with shock eliminations and a pandemic calling halt to proceedings.

What were all the dramas like on set?

A'WHORA: The show was the most unexpected, most on-edge experience of my life. When I walked into the werk room I looked around the room and thought, 'Joe Black is here,' who is a legend. Then Cherry Valentine, who had such

strong looks, went in episode 2, and then Asttina Mandella went in episode three. I mean, this is the girl who choreographed the Pussycat Dolls and danced with Christina Aguilera. Gone! I couldn't believe it. Every week was shocking.

A WINNER IS CHOSEN!

As season two headed towards its conclusion, viewers were divided over who should win. Lawrence was still a favourite, but Bimini and Tayce had gained a lot of fans over the last few episodes.

Were you sad not to win?

BIMINI: Obviously it's nice that people were really rooting for me. I went on the show, I nearly went home the first week and people saw that I really fought for it and I proved why I deserved to be there. I think after the non-binary chat with me and Ginny in episode three, people started really warming to me. And then we had the break and we came back for 'UK, Hun?' – everyone's mindset shifted. I didn't act up to the cameras. I didn't pretend to be anyone I wasn't. There was a bit of shading now and then, but it was always from a place of love. And I think that's why people got to like me. So the reactions I got from that were all I could have asked for.

'Life has given me so many things, so I want to give something back!'

Vanity Milan

Say hello, hello, hello to Ms Vanity Milan!

Lovely to meet you, Vanity. So, walking into the werk room for the first time must have been pretty sickening, right?

I walked in and was like, 'Wow, it's big, isn't it?' It's also cold, because the air conditioning is set to a really cold level and there I was, wearing this little costume, with my skin out, freezing. When I walked out, looking straight down that camera lens, I could feel my legs were shaking. But I was giving it full face, full Vanity Milan, full drama, full pose, full everything. It was my moment.

What did you make of your fellow queens?

Seeing Veronica Green was definitely exciting – I mean, welcome back, girl. And then I saw Kitty Scott-Claus, who I knew from one of my first drag competitions. There were a lot of queens that I was already following on social media such as River Medway, so I gushed, 'Oh my God, I love you.' we've now become really good friends. To be honest, we've all ended up becoming like a little family.

Season two had an edgier crew of queens. What did you make of them?

Seeing Asttina, Tayce and Tia, three people of colour, was definitely something that I liked. Asttina Mandella. I absolutely love her legs – she's just beautiful.

And there was also Bimini, just being an East-London "I just don't care gender bender". The conversation they had with Ginny Lemon about being non-binary was a pivotal moment. As a result, I think people – parents – understood a lot more about gender identity. It felt like such a genuine moment.

This season, *Drag Race UK* features the first AFAB queen, Victoria Scone!

When Victoria walked in, I was like, 'Jesus Christ. I've been following you for the longest time and now I get to meet you in person.'

Take us back to when you were a little boy. What was young Vanity Milan like?

Growing up is difficult for most of us, because you're trying to find yourself and your place in the world and work out what you want to do. For me, I was also suppressing feelings about who I was and getting bullied for it... So, growing up wasn't the easiest, but I always loved to dance, and I just chased my dream of performing. My parents never held me back and even took me to dance classes.

When did *Drag Race* enter your life?

RuPaul and *Drag Race* came at the time when I was working with a youth dance group. I'd ask my mum for money so I could go and buy wigs and she'd be like, 'What are you buying these things for?' And I'd be like, 'You'll understand when you watch *Drag Race*.' And now, all these years later, I'm on it. I can't believe it.

So how was Vanity Milan born?

She was born in the youth dance group, and she managed to get in quite a few performances, but when I moved to Estonia with my husband, I killed her off, and I stopped doing drag for a while. And then I said to my husband, 'I'm tired of living here in Estonia.' Luckily, he wanted to move back to London too, so when we got back I wanted to continue doing the dance thing. And then I took part in a competition that my friend was doing in 2019 and I revived Ms Vanity Milan for this competition, ended up winning, and I haven't stopped working since.

What's your post-*Drag Race* plan?

I'm going to hit the ground running. I'm going to give people joy, entertain and do as much as possible, because I have a family who I love to support. We've gone through a pandemic and people have lost jobs and specific things in life, and I'd like to give something back to them.

'Becoming
a performer
was always
something that
I wanted to do.'

Spill the Tia

Let's have a kiki!
The library is open!

Tia Kofi and her squirrel friends reveal what went on behind the scenes and what they really think of each other!

Tia dishes on her fellow queens! Miaow!

The meanest queen was ...

A'Whora. I never thought there was much to our spat until it became quite heated in that third episode, where thoughts and feelings and emotions came to the forefront and it really started to wear me down. In the fourth episode, I made that decision to take that Essex girl role after A'Whora selected it and initiate that deep conversation we had. I mean, A'Whora was very focused on fashion and appearance, while I was clearly not. But once we cleared the air and got those things out of the way, it all ultimately boiled down to us all being similar queer kids who have been judged and have had difficult times throughout our lives.

The warmest drag queen was . . .

Veronica Green, but I would also say Joe Black. Joe and I really bonded and that was really nice. Lawrence has also been a very warm and supportive queen.

CHIP SHOP CLASH

When two looks collided, who came out on top?

In season two, A'Whora and Sister Sister almost came to blows when they both wore a bag of chips on the runway! A'Whora was raging as she reckoned that Sister Sister had stolen her look. Sister, however, insisted it was just a coincidence. Who better to decide who wore it best than the nation's favourite Baga Chipz – er, Baga Chipz!

BAGA: I loved that they wanted to look like meeee! But when you saw them side by side you could see that A'Whora's Baga Chipz was better executed; it looked more polished and it looked more expensive, and, yeah, it was more rhinestoned. I'm glad I'm an inspirational fashion icon for the people.

WHEN CHERYL MET CHERYL

When an icon came face to face with their icon

If being on the world's greatest drag show wasn't enough for Cheryl Hole, then meeting an icon was just the cherry on the cake.

CHERYL: Everyone knew that I would be ecstatic about guest judge, Cheryl. After Ru announced it to the camera, he looked at me and said, 'Did you like that?' And I was like, 'What is happening?'

I think everybody expected me to have an emotional breakdown on the runway, but I knew I had to be composed. I mean, I'm not one to be screaming out someone's name at the stage door, but I perform in a Girls Aloud tribute group, and of course I'm named after Cheryl, so when I saw her, I held it together but inwardly I was amazed that I was getting to have this interaction. I think Cheryl was pleased that I was honouring the spirit of Girls Aloud – my runways paid homage to the Out of Control tour and the 'Untouchable' music video. I saw her again a while later at Manchester Pride and her PR person took me over to meet her and she was like, 'What the ...?' and gave me the biggest hug! She is so petite, so tiny – I thought I was going to break her.

Shady Blu Hydrangea casts her eye over the season one and season two queens' paint work!

BLU: Divina was always told on season one by Michelle that her face is grey, and I really did try to help her out as much as I could ... but nothing was helping her – that face, honestly! The only thing I could do was light a candle and say a prayer.

I love Baga with all my heart, but she went from wearing so much make-up in season one – like big brows and big lips – to now barely wearing any. I saw her do her make-up recently and she just put a little bit of blender on her beard area as if that's what she needed. I was like, 'Baga, babes, you need a cement truck full of foundation for that face!'

She's iconic, but I still to this day think about the make-up of hodgepodge queen Vinegar Strokes and think about how I'd fix it. I pray for her.

I think Tia Kofi has the bone structure to look like RuPaul. I'm also gonna say Ginny Lemon – although hers is a creative choice, I love to just beat her face.

How to Make Your Life Much Betta!

Your problems answered by Baga Chipz

Life ain't easy for any of us, so who better to solve our everyday problems than the queen of the battered sausage, Ms Baga Chipz, MBE?

'My boyfriend wants me to dress in drag all the time!'

Dear Baga,

I've been a drag queen for a few months and my boyfriend absolutely loves it. But recently he told me that he'd like me to dress up in drag all the time: in the bedroom, when we go out to the supermarket, when I'm making dinner. Is this normal? Or should I be worried?

Jamie, Newcastle

BAGA: I'm not putting my drag on to get a fella to like me! It's work, in't it! I mean, when a policeman goes home, he doesn't wear his uniform everywhere does he? People often say to me, 'Do you go to the shops dressed like that?' and I'm like, 'No!' I'm a performer – I wear my drag onstage, when I'm working. If I worked as a clown in a circus, I wouldn't go to the shop dressed as a clown with a big red bloody nose, would I?!

Dear Baga,

Drag Race has really inspired me to launch a career as a drag queen. I'm pretty funny and I have put together a fierce look, but I'm finding it hard to choose a great drag name! Can you help?

Michael, Manchester

BAGA: My advice is to choose a really unique name. We've already got so many Sandras and Crystals ... Pick something that's like, 'Wow!' People think I'm called Baga Chipz because I'm common and like chips, 'I go with anything' and I like to be covered in Daddies Sauce. But actually I got my name after some geezer tried to get in me and a mate's knickers on a night out. He was one of those cocky lads who thought he was the bollocks. So I said to him, 'Why would'ya wanna burger when I'm 100 per cent steak, sweetheart?' He looked me up and down and laughed. 'Prime steak? More like bag o' chips!' I was like, 'You cheeky bastard.' But it must have stuck with me cos Baga Chipz sounded just right for my Brummy tart with a heart. Some people have comedy names like Gonna Ria, but I'd say choose a name that represents you, maybe inspired by something that you love. So if your passion is gardening or flowers, maybe try Ms Penis FlyTrap.

'Should I clean up my dirty drag act for my parents?'

Dear Baga,

I've been a drag queen for a couple of years. Recently my parents told me they wanted to come and see my show for the first time. Now, as you can imagine, my show is filthy. Should I clean up my act for my parents or should I just give them what I normally do?

Chris, Birmingham

BAGA: Just tell your family it's all a big act. It's acting, it's a performance. I'm playing a character. Everything I'm saying is a joke. It's like Joan Rivers – she would say the most offensive things onstage, but it was all just an act.

'How can I come out to my boyfriend as a drag queen?'

Dear Baga,

I have been doing drag for the past few weeks. I have just started dating a new guy, who says that he hates drag queens. How am I possibly going to tell him that I am one? I don't want to lose him!

Marcos, Lee

BAGA: Just show them a picture of Baga Chipz and your boyfriend will have a massive erection! And then he'll probably dump yer and go out wi' me. Seriously, if he likes you for you, then he'll stick by yer.

Dear Baga,

I am a new queen on the block and am trying to slowly build my drag kit! What should every queen carry around with them at all times?

Chris, Brixton

'What should I carry around in my drag bag?'

BAGA: You must always carry a lippy or a lip gloss, cos if you have a drink when you're out it's just gonna come right off. A compact powder is a must to give yourself a touch-up! When you're onstage you sweat your bollocks off and afterwards you end up looking in the mirror thinking, 'I've got no make-up on!' Always have your phone on yer to get an Uber home. I know people like to go on the train and the Tube, but we don't live in *The Wizard of Oz*, we live in a world where people get attacked and stuff. Don't be getting on tubes and buses on your own in full drag! I'm not saying you shouldn't be allowed. I'm just saying, in a realistic world, I want everyone to be safe. Clowns get ready at work.

'Drag queens are talking about me behind my back!'

Dear Baga,

I'm pretty new on the drag scene and have made a few friends – or so I thought. I recently discovered that some of the girls are talking about me. What should I do?

Gareth, Stockwell

BAGA: The best form of revenge is success. You don't want toxic people or jealousy round yer. Surround yourself with people who are rooting for you and who are championing you. If you've got people who are gonna throw you under a bus, just get rid, and when you're successful and famous like me, they'll all be back, licking your arse! I've had thousands of queens criticise me, but I don't acknowledge them. They're beneath me. I've got very thick skin. I'm one of them people who doesn't give a crap what people think about me, as long as I'm still living the celebrity lifestyle I live, and enjoying life as one of the most famous women in Britain. And I still have Princess Diana's cheekbones, so I'm 'appy.

'How can I handle hecklers?'

Dear Baga,

I really love my life as a drag queen, but even though I enjoy entertaining the crowds, when someone starts to heckle me from the crowd it really throws me off my stride. What can I do?

Julian, Clapham

BAGA: If you get a heckler, you just say, 'Stop the music.' Make that person feel tiny. If they want to play Billy Big Bollocks, show 'em that you're ten times bigger. You're onstage putting on some entertainment. Most of these places are free to get in. You just say to them, 'If you don't like it, there's a Toby Carvery up the road. Now get lost!'

'I wore a dress to prom!'

Meet the Queens confessionals

Say hello to fabulous Brighton-based queen Anubis . . .

Condragulations for making it onto season three. Was this your first attempt?

I had been waiting to apply since I was 15. So once I was legally allowed to, I sent in that form.

You must have been gagged!

At 19, I'm one of the youngest contestants that has ever been on the franchise, but I've always been an old soul, with an older head on a younger body, so I think for me the time does feel right, as I feel like I've waited a lifetime for this to happen.

How did you first discover *Drag Race*?

I was about 12. The first queen I remember falling in love with was Bianca Del Rio – I was amazed at just how witty and quick she was. She was so cutting and she was so able to deliver the jokes in such a unique way that I'd never seen before, especially at such a young age. She really inspired me. So I think that was the turning point for me, when I realised that drag could be a career that isn't just putting on a lash and rocking up to the club.

Did you know you were different at this stage in your life?

I came out as bi when I was ten, which I guess is rather young. I actually came out in the backseat of the car on the way to a Toby Carvery. That was quite fun. My mum just said to me, 'Don't be so greedy.' At the time I was very confused and I was very sceptical about how the rest of my family would react, because I was so young and felt they might think it was just a phase and all those other things that you always get told.

You lost a massive nine stone. What impact did that have on you?

I used to eat my emotions and to some degree I think I still do. The reason I wanted to lose the weight was because I would wake up every day and look in the mirror for the person who I knew I was deep down. But I never saw him looking back. I felt physically, spiritually and mentally drained. That was why I wanted to lose some weight. I didn't realise that it was going to be nine stone in a year. I did it by changing my diet and dancing

What kind of queen is Anubis?

She was born out of a love for theatre and wacky, weird Dr Seuss characters. But she was fully realised through music.

How do you think *Drag Race* has changed the lives of young people in the LGBTQ+ community and changed people's perceptions?

I think it's changed everything in terms of the LGBTQ+ community. I think everyone's outlook is different. The language that is involved now – people are having conversations about non-binary people or AFAB queens. I don't think a wider audience would know all this new terminology without *Drag Race*. The 'British gay icon' episode in season two, when Tayce and Asttina, after realising they've both chosen Naomi Campbell for their runway look have a conversation about how they didn't really have many options to choose from, being people of colour – even conversations like that, about racism, homophobia, or gender identity – this show has allowed those conversations to happen, while showcasing 12 creative, incredible people and having a laugh while doing it. That's why the show is so successful and people gravitate towards it. It's just fun to watch and you get educated on really important subjects.

Drag Race UK Translations

Still not got a clue what the Brit queens are going on about in their wacky seasons? Now you can.

After more than a decade of the original *RuPaul's Drag Race*, drag slang has become part of our everyday chat! Even your grandma is banging on about her back rolls and exclaiming 'Yas Queen!' while sashaying down an Aldi aisle.

But our UK divas have brought their own special flavour to the iconic series that international fans may have found hard to get their heads around.

Here's an easy to grasp glossary of Brit Drag Lingo used during the first two seasons of *Drag Race UK*.

Battered sausage – A tasty but not entirely healthy sausage that is fried in batter and is traditionally served in fish and chip shops. Of course, Baga delights in using the phrase in the filthiest of ways!

Bender – This word has two meanings. One is when you are referring to getting wasted on a big night out, ('We're going out on a bender!'), and the other is a homophobic slur that LGBTQ+ folk occasionally reclaim and use in humour.

Coronation Street – Baga mentions the iconic 61-year old soap in her workroom entrance. It's a gritty soap set in the north of England, which in its early days featured a series of camp, brassy women who have greatly inspired the Birmingham queen.

Daddies Sauce – Another of Baga's saucy catchphrases. In reality this is a tasty brown sauce used to accompany food but obviously in Baga's drag context, it has a filthier connotation.

Gobby / Gob shite – A loud, brash and outspoken person. Er.... Baga anyone?

Kim Woodburn – TV Cleaner and reality star whose iconic pulled back pony and outrageous put down and catchphrases has made her a UK legend.

Mystic Meg – Popular British fortune teller from the 90s who used to predict who would win the National Lottery. Best known for her relaxing voice and incredibly angular black bob!

On the piss – Getting very drunk on a wild night out.

Sacka Spudz – The drag name of Baga's mum in the make over episode. The name refers to a cloth bag that contains potatoes, the vegetable which can be cut into chips too!

Trollop – This old-fashioned term refers to someone who enjoys having it away with the lads – however, due to its vintage origins, it's also considered as another way of saying 'hot mess'.

Tuppence – In years gone by, a tuppence was an old British coin. Nowadays it's a used as slang for vagina.

'You Ain't My Muvva' – Quote used by Bimini and RuPaul in season two comes from a now iconic scene from popular TV soap *Eastenders* in which characters Zoe Slater tells her 'sister' Kat that she's not her mother, only for Kat to finally reveal that she is indeed the woman who gave birth to her! Ooh the drama!

'I am the spiciest, meatiest, silliest sausage on the drag scene!'

Say 'Hola' to the UK-based Spanish queen Choriza May . . .

Welcome to *Drag Race*, Choriza. You must be thrilled.

I am. It is like a dream come true and it's been a lot of fun.

You were born in Spain, but you have lived in Newcastle for years, right?

Yes, I moved to the UK almost six years ago for uni and I started doing drag two and a half years ago. And that's where Choriza May came to life. Choriza is the spiciest, meatiest and silliest sausage on the drag scene.

What is Choriza May about?

I mostly lip sync, but what I do is normally pick quite a few songs and try to tell a story or make a political point. One of my biggest inspirations is Sasha Velour. I love how she just takes a song and a [few] spoken words tells you a completely new story.

What was growing up in Spain like?

I grew up in a very, very small town in Valencia. It was very isolated. We didn't have a train station. I basically grew up in a place where I thought there was no way out for me. I liked boys and I was asking myself, 'Why is this happening to me?' None of my friends were attracted to boys. I didn't know any gay couples. I didn't have any gay relatives. I didn't have anyone.

Were your parents okay about it?

Well, my mum was, but my dad pretended to be. Because I was so very young, they told me just to forget about it and focus on school with friends. When I was 18, I brought my first boyfriend home and things got a little bit bad with my dad, but he never told me he was angry at me or that he didn't accept it. I just felt he didn't like me.

Did he eventually come to terms with it?

I studied around the world so removed myself from the situation. My dad is a fairly laddie kind of guy, so I think I had to prove to him by working really hard that being gay was not going to affect my career. So I worked hard to prove I was just as capable of doing as well as all the straight kids in my class, and did even better.

So he likes Choriza?

He's the biggest Choriza May fan ever. He saw me perform in Spain before COVID. He and Mum got the train to visit me in Madrid to see my show in a bar and I could see he was very proud. So it was very nice.

'Never in a million years would I have thought I would end up on that show. It's really crazy.'

When did you move to the UK?

When I was a student I came to Newcastle for six months and learned English. Newcastle is not the best place to learn English. To start with I didn't understand a word of what my lecturers were saying. Thankfully, I managed to get a ... well, I wouldn't say a boyfriend ... but a buddy who was an English teacher and would correct all my assignments. And that's how I managed to get through the six months. I had no idea what I was doing.

So when you first saw *Drag Race* did it have a big impact on you?

The first time that I saw it was season six when I was in Brazil. I had lots of free time and I didn't have many friends because I had just started at the uni. And then I discovered Detox and was just mesmerised. She was so beautiful. I was like, 'What is this?' And then I started watching, watching, watching. Never in a million years would I have thought I would end up on that show. It's really crazy.

At Home With A'Whora and Tayce

What really goes on behind closed doors!

During the lockdown break in season two, sassy bezzas A'Whora and Tayce shacked up together in a London pad. Now, in a classic glossy celeb-weekly style-at-home spread, we visit the girls' glamazon pad and ask A'Whora exactly what everyday life is like at Casa T'Whora!

So spill the tea, A'Whora, which of you is the messiest in the house?

Tayce is a walking tornado. Anything she walks past, it just falls off or smashes. She's just an absolute hound. Honestly, you can't leave her anywhere. I dread to think what she's like in a restaurant, because she'd turn a table upside down.

Which of you whips out the Mr Muscle and does the tidying up?

We actually have a cleaner. She comes every Friday. She sorts out all of Tayce's mess, thank God!

Who has the most clothes in their wardrobe?

Me! I'm a bloody nightmare. I've got bin bags full of clothes. I live in the loft, so I've got a full storage unit just for all my clothes. I'm an absolute hoarder. I'll buy something and I can't get rid of it because I get so emotionally attached to it. I also tend to keep all the stuff I have designed – even the stuff I did for school and college projects. The outfit that Tayce wore for the prehistoric runway – the jumper with the claw – I made that when I was 16 at college.

Who spends most time in the bathroom?

We actually have our own en suites, darling. So we never really see each other. But I do have a tendency to go for a little 'one-two' and I'll be sat there for about seven hours just watching myself on YouTube and absolutely enjoying the moment.

What irritates you most about each other?

Tayce can go all diva sometimes and thinks she can tell me what to do. She'll always ask to borrow my stuff, but whenever I ask to borrow something, she'll go, 'No!' And I'm like, 'Er, okay, so last week you borrowed my tracksuit, my wig and blah-blah-blah and that wasn't a problem?' We argue about stuff like that all the time. What else do we argue about? Sharing stuff. She's a joke with that. She never buys the essentials. She never buys bread. She won't buy milk. She won't buy coffee or washing-up liquid or bin bags – you know, the basics. And then she'll pipe up and say, 'Why are there no bin bags?' And I'll say,

'Well, maybe if you went and got some, you idiot.' I think she thinks they just magically appear.

Do you often see your infamous nan?

She died watching the episode! Just joking. She's fully with us.

Have you always been very close to her?

I was put into care when I was 13 and she got custody of me and raised me from 13 to 18, when I moved to London. So when I was asked about relationships on the show, the only ones I've ever had were my ex-boyfriend or my nan. She basically gave me a second chance at life and pushed me to do what I do.

You and your nan seem to have a great bond.

Me and my nan sit for hours watching Catherine Tate's 'Nan'. It was very much our sense of humour. So when I did the stand-up challenge on the show, I thought I'd play on this nan vibe and just roll with it. I thought it was going to be hilarious and I'd end up with my own stand-up show – but everyone disagreed.

Everybody loves Bingo

Become part of the show!

Now we all know it's a hoot watching any episode of *Drag Race* but wouldn't it be great if you could feel even more part of the show. Below are four bingo cards for you and some friends to mark off as you watch an episode.

The first to cry 'Bingo Bom Boulash' is the winner. If by the end of the episode no one has called out, then the player with the most boxes marked off wins!

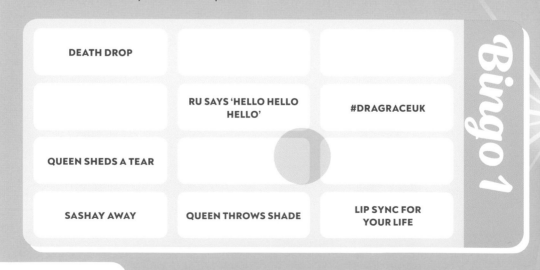

DEATH DROP		
	RU SAYS 'HELLO HELLO HELLO'	#DRAGRACEUK
QUEEN SHEDS A TEAR		
SASHAY AWAY	QUEEN THROWS SHADE	LIP SYNC FOR YOUR LIFE

Bingo 1

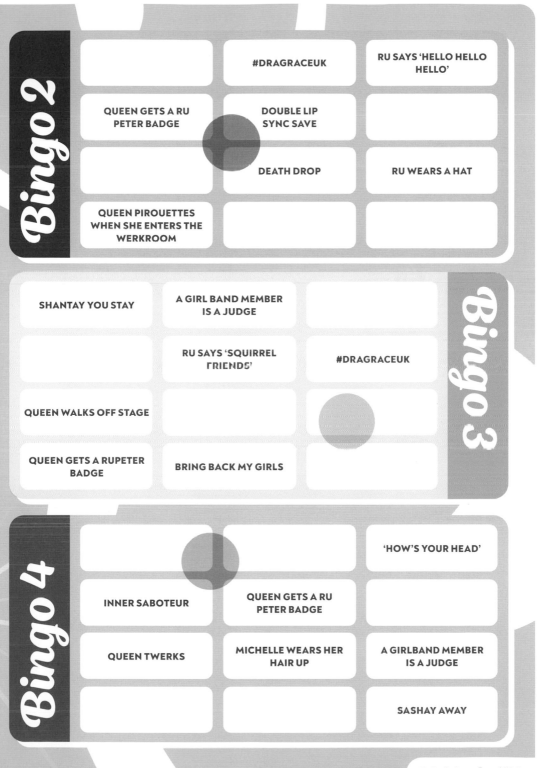

Bingo 2

	#DRAGRACEUK	RU SAYS 'HELLO HELLO HELLO'
QUEEN GETS A RU PETER BADGE	DOUBLE LIP SYNC SAVE	
	DEATH DROP	RU WEARS A HAT
QUEEN PIROUETTES WHEN SHE ENTERS THE WERKROOM		

Bingo 3

SHANTAY YOU STAY	A GIRL BAND MEMBER IS A JUDGE	
	RU SAYS 'SQUIRREL FRIENDS'	#DRAGRACEUK
QUEEN WALKS OFF STAGE		
QUEEN GETS A RUPETER BADGE	BRING BACK MY GIRLS	

Bingo 4

		'HOW'S YOUR HEAD'
INNER SABOTEUR	QUEEN GETS A RU PETER BADGE	
QUEEN TWERKS	MICHELLE WEARS HER HAIR UP	A GIRLBAND MEMBER IS A JUDGE
		SASHAY AWAY

'I'm not going to let a single thing get in my way.'

Meet the Queens confessionals

Scarlett Harlett

He calls himself 'the Danny Dyer of drag'. Meet East-End queen Scarlett Harlett.

Well done for making it onto season three! Have you always been a big *Drag Race* fan?

The biggest! I know the exact moment that I came across it. I was in college – so around 16, 17 – and season four [of the US show] had just aired. I was scrolling on one of the computers in the media room and came across the reunion episode. I thought to myself, 'Oh my God, this has to be the weirdest Real Housewives show I've ever seen in my life.' I've loved it ever since. It was an eye-opening experience. It was amazing to see all these queer people on TV. I was the only openly gay person in my school or college, so I didn't have any gay friends, so watching the show was amazing. It was like, these are my people, my tribe.

So how did Scarlett Harlett come about?

I'd seen *Drag Race* and didn't have a clue what I was doing, so I looked up [US drag queen] Manila Luzon's make-up tutorial. I watched that religiously, over and over again. I bought all of the products that she had and spent the next six to eight months just practising my make-up. I still have pictures that I took from when I first started – I look rough. I spent a couple of months in my dorm at uni learning how to do my make-up, then decided I was good enough to get out there and show my face in public and entered a little drag competition called So You think You Can Drag? I lip synced and won the competition!

Did you end up performing in any bars?

I did a bit of TV for a while, including a music video with Danny Dyer called 'Nebraska' [by Lucy Rose], in which he plays a drag queen. And what's funny is, I call myself 'the Danny Dyer of drag'.

You once said that you never thought a UK *Drag Race* could work …

I was absolutely baffled at how they were going to do it. I mean, the UK drag scene is so small, or at least it was at the time. I remember thinking, 'If they're going to stick to this American formula of having lip-sync queens and all of that, they're going to run out of a pool of queens very quickly.' But I think the first season was done exceptionally well.

So what was walking into the werk room like?

It felt like I was in another world. It's funny – when we're filming, I'd go back to the hotel and watch season two on the TV and it didn't feel like I was a part of what I was watching, even though it's exactly the same thing. It didn't feel real. The second I walked into the werk room I felt like this was my moment. And I thought, 'You know what? I'm not going to let a single thing get in my way.'

Which of the queens did you bond with most?

Kitty Scott-Claus is hilarious and the sweetest person ever. Not a bad word came out of her mouth. I don't know how you can be a drag queen and be like that. She's just so genuine and sweet and easy to get along with.

'It felt like I was in another world.'

The Snatch Game

Secrets

QUEENS' SNATCH ADVICE

1) Pick someone who's already put the work in

BAGA CHIPZ: Bimini's Katie Price was genius, but she's quite easy to do – you just don't pronounce your Rs. You say 'Pwice' and 'pwincess' and 'in the pwess' and it's all just very pouty. 'When I was a page "fwee" model ...' You know what I mean? She is a perfect person to do. Don't pick someone where you have to put too much work in. Pick someone who's already done it for you. Pick someone ridiculous and then you've only got to say what they've done.

2) Avoid talented people

BAGA CHIPZ: Don't pick people like make-up gurus or Beyoncé or Mariah Carey or Lady Gaga. They're talented people, but they're not funny. Is Lady Gaga funny? She's serious! It would be like playing someone like Angela Bassett – she's a serious actress.

3) Research your character

CHERYL HOLE: Choose someone loud and big and ridiculous so you can ham it up. If you play someone reserved like Posh Spice, all you can do is: 'David and I have five kids. I've got a fashion line.' I'd suggest you research the person, know them inside and out. If they have a husband, when did they get married? What was their wedding dress like? Watch all their TV shows. Pick their best bits. Find their nuances and their ridiculous moments that you can make your own. It's one thing quoting a moment, but you have to make it funny and give it your own spin. Bimini did it best – she paraphrased Katie's rant about being held up at gun point, and it was hysterical. Doing funny things like that will take you far.

4) Be clever

BAGA CHIPZ: When BenDeLaCreme did Maggie Smith in the US series, it was really funny, but she was playing her like a character. She's an American queen playing a funny British character. It really showed off BenDeLaCreme's acting ability. Even her improvisation was brilliant – when someone said, 'Can you get this person to speak English?' she said, 'We originated the language!' Gigi Goode's robot was risky but really clever, and you'd never think of doing that either.

BIMINI: WHY I DID KATIE PRICE

When Bimini took her seat on the Snatch Game panel as hunty glamour girl Katie Price, viewers were gagged! But why did Bim choose Katie?

I have always loved Katie Price. I grew up watching her and I always thought she was just so interesting as a character. She was a glamour model who put herself out there for the male gaze. But Katie monetised every opportunity she got and became a successful businesswoman, making all those deals that no glamour model had really done before. She became her own kind of entity. People mocked her, people ripped into her, but she was doing it for her children. Look at everything she's done for her son Harvey and her kids – she loves and adores them. She's been scrutinised so much by the British media, who tend to target successful women and try to bring them down. She's seen as very lowbrow, but she's actually a smart woman, and I just think that's why I did it. My Snatch Game was from a place of love. I've watched her as I've grown up, so I knew the way she speaks and her mannerisms, and what I tried to embody with Katie is that you never know what is going to come out of her mouth. Thankfully, when she watched it she got it, cos she can take the piss out of herself and she saw I wasn't doing it maliciously. Also, Katie is a bit like us a drag queen. A lot of females that are in the limelight are drag queens, just without the label. Ask any gay man who they are inspired by and they'll say Madonna, Cher and all of these people. They're all drag queens, essentially.

'Drag Race UK *feels fresh.* British queens, British jokes and that I-don't-give-a-damn vibe!'

Krystal Versace

Oi-oi! Say hello to Ms Krystal Versace from Kent, who chats about being a cheeky teen, how he discovered drag and becoming a Drag Race queen!

When you found out you'd got on the show, how did that feel?

It was crazy. Looking back, when I was filling out the form, I thought I might have to wait until season five, cos I was just 19. But then I thought, 'Why not give it a go?' So I did. As I became more invested in it and sent off my video, I had a feeling in my gut that something was going to happen. And then we got the call just before Christmas and it was amazing. The brain started working 300 miles an hour, thinking overtime. So I quickly got all my stuff together.

What's it like walking into the werk room?

It was crazy – it was the most nerve-wracking thing. It was so scary. I remember it being so silent. I was second to last going in. I had never been on TV before, so turning that corner into the room was a shock, as I had never seen so many cameras before.

For the Snatch Game, did you know who you might do?

I knew who I'd planned to do. I love doing accents and have a laugh quoting people. I'm good at improvising. I'm not a comedy queen, but I don't take things seriously. I was like, 'Give it your best shot.'

Were you a quiet kid?

Not at all! I was always the one with the mouth. If a teacher had something to say then they could expect a reply. I was pretty feisty. When I started to own who I was, I was like, 'You can't tell me nothing.' I grew up in a Christian school – there were a few boundaries that were crossed with me. School wasn't great.

When did the make-up turn into doing drag?

So I was really keen to become a make-up artist and this was at a time when *Drag Race* was blowing up. I would try drag make-up, cos it looked really great. Now and then I would dabble in it, then a wig would come in, then a heel came in and then it became a thing and I thought, 'This is really cool.'

And the name? Is it an homage to Michelle Visage's favourite film, *Showgirls*?

I liked the name Versace because it sounded expensive, it sounded cute, and then this boy I was talking to suggested I add Crystal. I thought Crystal Versace had a ring to it, it was cute, so I was like, 'Let's go.' But when I tried to set myself up on Instagram someone already had it, so I changed the 'C' to a 'K'!

'I had never been on TV before, so turning that corner into the room was a shock.'

The Charisma, Uniqueness, Nerve and Talent Quiz

Which of these sexy qualities best sums you up?

Charisma, Uniqueness, Nerve, and Talent: the four key qualities that Ru and the judges are looking for in a queen.

But which of these sickening qualities do YOU exhibit most? Take the below quiz to find out! For some extra fun, can you name the queen that wore each outfit?

1

Michelle Visage invites you to the launch night of her band Seduction's reunion tour. What do you wear to upstage her?

A. A black and green suit with rainbow binary code on it
B. A yellow polka dot seagull bathing suit with orange webbed heels
C. A regal robe and feathered cap with a lingerie reveal
D. A black and red striped latex mermaid gown

2

The GC is interviewing for a new PA – how would you dress to impress?

A. A yellow 60s flower print dress, neon yellow tights and yellow platform foam slippers
B. A hodge-podge blazer and mini skirt made from book pages and... nipple tassles?
C. A Norwich football leotard with shiny black thigh-high platform boots
D. A blue plastic superhero gown with ruffled sleeves and a metal corset

3

Jourdan Dunn asks you to share the catwalk with her – which of these looks would you wear to outshine her?

A. A white rose-print face-kini with green bows and a massive matching hat
B. A red and cream dress with a blue eyeball helmet
C. A pink facemask leotard combo with two Sai daggers
D. A laundry bag checked pantsuit with a red and white parasol

4

Geri Horner has asked you to babysit Bluebell for a couple of hours. Which of these outfits fits the bill?

A. A pink dress with a big bow on the back with pink heels with bows on them
B. A floral dress with gingerbread cookies to hide your true robot form underneath
C. A yellow and black polka-dot dress with a black balloon
D. A gold and green ballgown with matching crown

5

Alan Carr has asked you to take his pet pooches for a walk. Which of these garments makes you feel your oats?

A. A black pinstripe blazer with tiger face paint
B. A long white dress and a giant first-class stamp
C. An orange and silver latex dress with a flotation device hat
D. A black full-length dress with big shoulder pads made from VHS tape

6

RuPaul is looking for someone to pick up his designer suits from the dry cleaner's. What easy look do you grab from your wardrobe?

A. A sparkly black sequined suit with a bowler hat
B. A tiger-print dress with green tassels, bone mask, and a tall blonde wig
C. A metallic collared bodysuit with matching thigh high boots
D. A green, white and red feathered dress with a dragon's face

MAINLY As

You are absolutely bursting with CHARISMA. There's something absolutely sickening about you that makes people fall under your spell. Wherever you go, you turn heads (maybe a few tricks) and captivate anyone in a room. Maybe it's that sickening personality of yours.

MAINLY Bs

Bless you, chuck. UNIQUENESS is your middle name and no mistake. No one on God's good earth could accuse you of following the crowd. No siree! You're a kook and then some. And that is what makes you such a great person. Fancy a slice?

MAINLY Cs

Well, well, well, you fierce fox, you. Barely wearing any of those fleshy outfits and even daring to step out of the house looking that fine proves you have a lot of NERVE. You're not scared to make a statement, to walk into a room purse first or stand out from the crowd! You're a pioneer and you will always be one of life's tops (unless you love to be a bottom).

MAINLY Ds

Hey girl, you are not resting on pretty or ugly. You're resting on brains, queen! You are a TALENT-serving Glamazon who doesn't need a season one filter to look good. When you put your mind to something, you just do it. You're creative. An expert in all that you do, the kind of queen that can dominate a mini or maxi challenge and walk away with a RuPeter badge or three.

Er ... ALL OF THEM?

Well, of course, girls, in reality, we possess all four qualities. That's because we are all fierce quadruple-threat queens who own everything. We have sass, individuality, guts and skills that make us different to the next person. Always remember that. Just look at yourself in the mirror and serve up your best inner queen. Can we get an amen up in here?

ANSWERS

1a Tia Kofi, 1b Ellie Diamond, 1c Divina de Campo, 1d Ellie Diamond, 2a Ginny Lemon, 2b Vinegar Strokes, 2c Bimini Bon-Boulash, 2d A'Whora, 3a Crystal, 3b Bblu Hydrangea, 3c Asttina Mandella, 3d Divina de Campo, 4a Scaredy Kat, 4b Veronica Green, 4c Cherry Valentine, 4d Joe Black, 5a Gothy Kendoll, 5b Sum Ting Wong, 5c Lawrence Chaney, 5d The Vivienne, 6a Baga Chipz, 6b Sister Sister, 6c Cheryl Hole, 6d Tayce.

'I actually feel more self-conscious when I'm in drag!'

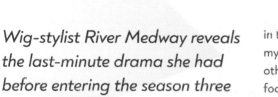

River Medway

Wig-stylist River Medway reveals the last-minute drama she had before entering the season three werk room.

Condragulations, River, on making it onto season three! You must be living your best life.

I am, actually. It was my first time auditioning. I had done so much drag in lockdown – I mean, what else was I gonna do?

As your name suggests, you grew up in Kent. What was young River Medway like?

I have always been an ethnic minority, as where I live is a very white town. When I was at school, around five or six years old, I had a few incidents with a mean racist girl who made me realise that I was different to everyone else. Before that, I never looked

in the mirror and saw anything other than myself. I began to realise I wasn't like all the other boys at school. I didn't like playing football. I liked playing with the girls and doing handstands on the fields and doing cartwheels and singing Kylie Minogue. People really liked me because I'm talkative, I am very friendly. I make people laugh a lot. People thought I was funny and a bit weird. I went to an all-boys grammar school and there was no one quite like me. I had friends, but we were the outcasts and we became friends because we didn't fit into all the groups.

Were your family supportive?

Very much so. I have a sister who is four years older than me and she introduced me to the Spice Girls, Destiny's Child, Britney, Mariah. I think she's the reason I'm a drag queen, as we'd be at home putting on shows for our parents every week. I have not grown up at all. I am the same person I was at five years old. My mum, who sadly passed away recently, influenced me too – she was a huge David Bowie fan and told me how at 15 she would dye her hair and shave off her eyebrows and draw them back on with funny colours. Also my dad has always said, 'Be whatever you want, as long as you are happy.' I'm so glad I got into this year's *Drag Race* – I felt like I was doing it for my mum. I knew she'd be so proud of me.

When was River Medway born?

I used to steal my sister's dresses and try them on in the bathroom. Nobody ever knew. I was obsessed with her blue sequin dress. Then, when I was seven, I bought a red wig from Poundland for Halloween and I became totally obsessed with it. I love wigs so much. I don't know what it is about them, but I absolutely love them. When I was about 14, I wanted to start doing the female roles at my youth theatre. It was so great, as it was such an escape from boring normal life. So all my references for drag were from theatre and panto dames, so traditional British cross-dressing.

How did the show impact on you?

I binged on season six [of the US series] and was just so bewildered that the show had been going on for six seasons without me knowing about it. I kind of knew RuPaul, cos I knew 'Supermodel (You Better Work)'. And I only knew that because it appears on the *Lizzie Maguire Movie* soundtrack, sung by Taylor Dayne. I loved it, looked it up and found out that someone called RuPaul had recorded it first. So I became a bit of a fangirl, obviously. When you are young and queer, it's great to see people like me doing something with drag, not just being a panto dame doing the bingo. When I was watching *Drag Race* and saw all these people who had grown up like me, I noticed there were so many similarities! We all thought we were alone, that we were the only ones in the world like this, then you grow up and realise that you weren't.

Many people say they see drag as a suit of armour.

I actually think the opposite. I feel more self-conscious. I am so critical of myself that when I am in drag I feel exposed and vulnerable because I'm showing off my make-up and hair skills. If people judge my face out of drag, I don't care, because I can't do anything about that!

What was it like when Ru walked in? It was like watching TV.

I actually screamed. I couldn't believe it was RuPaul in the flesh – he never felt like a real person, but more of an entity to me. I was just standing there – thinking 'What is going on?'

And what was your first runway like?

All of a sudden, the competition felt real and I remember feeling really awful about my outfit. It didn't feel good enough. I just sat there before the first runway wondering why I was putting myself through this.

Wow! How did you manage to pull yourself together?

I knew that if I was going to survive the first week, then my personality would have to get me through. So when I came down the runway, I added some silly moves. I can't tell you how relieved and happy I was when I saw that Ru and the judges were laughing really hard. They liked me!

Canada

Drag Race alumna Brooke Lynn Hytes joined Stacey McKenzie and Jeffrey Bowyer-Chapman to judge the drag talents of Canadians and chose Priyanka as the series' first winner. In January 2021, Season 2 was officially announced!

UK

It took ten years, but the UK finally got its own show, with RuPaul at the helm, ably assisted by Michelle Visage, Graham Norton and Alan Carr. The show proved to be one of BBC Three's most successful shows EVER!

USA

Since it launched in 2009, there have been 13 series of *Drag Race*, six series of *All Stars Untucked*, Christmas special *RuPaul's Drag Race Holi-slay Spectacular* and a star-studded *RuPaul's Secret Celebrity Drag Race*.

Spain

Another spin-off arrived in 2021, this time in sunny Spain, and the gorgeous Supremme de Luxe managed to slip into Ru's heels to take on hosting duties. Season 2 is also on the way!

Who'd have thought that back in 2009 a small competition with little-known drag queens would captivate the world the way RuPaul's Drag Race *has. Well, it did, and countries across the globe lapped up the US series and its spin-offs like* Untucked!, All Stars *and* Secret Celebrity Drag Race. *Keen for their own shows, some countries have produced amazing versions!*

Chile

The earliest of the international versions, *The Switch Drag Race* first aired in 2015, with a second series in 2018, and was hosted by Karla Constant.

Wonder

RuPaul really does rule the world!

Holland

In September 2020, Holland launched its own *Drag Race*, presented by the sensational Fred van Leer. After weeks of wild shenanigans and lips synch, Envy Peru was crowned drag superstar. The second season of *Drag Race Holland* premiered in August 2021.

Philippines

On August 16 World of Wonder officially announced that the Filipino series will also be joining the *Drag Race* family, introducing audiences to the dazzling queens of the Philippines.

Italy

Officially confirmed by World of Wonder, *Drag Race Italia* will premiere in 2021 hosted by Chiara Francini, Priscilla and Tommaso Zorzi.

Australia and New Zealand

With *RDR* having been a huge hit Down Under, it was only a matter of time before the countries had a show of its own – and Ru and Michelle were along for the ride. The cast were revealed in spectacular style at the Sydney Mardi Gras in March!

Thailand

Although Ru isn't a host on this hugely popular version of the show, it was one of the first international series to appear. So far, just two series have aired, which were co-hosted by Art Arya and Pangina Heals, who crowned Natalia Pliacam in 2018 and Angele Anang the year after.

DRAGCON UK 2020

At the start of 2020, a host of international drag superstars descended on Olympia London to meet and greet the drag fans of the United Kingdom and enchant them with their charisma, uniqueness, nerve and talent.

The thousands of fans who had descended on the historic expo hall were treated to a sickening runway strut by *Drag Race* alumni and the cast of *Drag Race UK*.

Of course, a queen's only at her best when she's werking a crowd, so when The Vivienne and Cheryl Hole (introduced onstage by Tina from S Club 7, no less) took to the stage to sing and lip sync, the crowd practically exploded.

However, when the Frock Destroyers took their turn to perform it was like the Spice Girls had reformed and you could barely hear them slay their smash-hit single 'Break Up (Bye Bye)' for the cheering.

THE VIVIENNE TAKES ON HOLLYWOOD

Each week the UK queens competed for coveted RuPeter badges and the chance to star in their own digital series produced by World of Wonder.

After season one wrapped, The Vivienne jetted out to the World of Wonder studios in Hollywood to shoot her first ever pop video.

MORNING T&T

When Baga and The Vivienne stole the season one Snatch Game with their impersonations of former world leaders Margaret Thatcher and Donald Trump, the world was gagged. Not only did Michelle Visage think The Viv's Trump was the best she'd ever seen, fellow judge Alan Carr suggested that the two characters needed their own spin-off show. Well, the folks at World of Wonder had also spotted the brilliant banter between the pair and no sooner had season one wrapped than Baga and Viv were filming an outrageous mini web series, once again playing the notorious politicians.

Wish You Were Queer

The international winners of Drag Race in Canada, Chile and Thailand on how the show changed their lives and what they thought of the UK series!

Priyanka, winner of Canada's Drag Race

In 2020, the former kids' TV presenter became Canada's first ever drag superstar!

The UK series proved to be really popular outside of the UK. In Canada and America does UK culture still have an impact?

The UK version made such an impact. All my friends watched it. My friends talked about it. It was all we cared about because it was another *Drag Race* to watch. So it definitely impacted here. I'm begging for the UK girls to come over here because I want to see them perform live.

Were you surprised that the UK series did so well globally?

The biggest bands in the world come from the UK, I was like, the UK is full of stars waiting to explode, so there's no way we're not going to like this, and those accents are just so damn charming! We love a British accent. Some people even change [the voice of] Siri on their phone to have a British accent!

LEONA WINTER, winner of The Switch

Formerly known as Miss Leona, the French drag superstar was crowned the winner of the second season of the Chilean version of the show.

What is your advice to aspiring queens?

You have to be kind to others and stay true to yourself. The most important thing is to believe in yourself and do everything – to never regret anything.

Who has been your favourite UK drag queen and why?

I lived for Bimini Bon-Boulash! She is a really talented queen, fierce and beautiful. I loved her looks and make-up. She surprised me with unexpected and original proposals.

Angele Anang, winner of season two of Drag Race Thailand

Angele made herstory by becoming the franchise's first transgender drag superstar!

How did you feel when you won? How has your life changed?

Being a drag queen is not just about fabulous hair or dresses, but who I am. I really appreciate that. The platform really could change the world.

What is your advice to aspiring queens?

Be you. Embrace who you are. Make it your energy.

Who was your favourite UK drag queen and why?

Sum Ting Wong, because she's my friend and she's the funny one.

She Said What?

As we all know, almost everything that comes out our UK queens' mouths is iconic, mama.

Here are a make-up bagful of sassy quotes from the queens of seasons one and two.

But can you remember who said what?

Start your engines, and may the best reader win!

But our UK divas have brought their own special flavour to the iconic series that international fans may have found hard to get their heads around.
    Here's an easy to grasp glossary of Brit Drag Lingo used during the first two seasons of *Drag Race UK*.

1

Which queen uttered these, er, touching words about Cheryl Hole?

'I'm in the bottom! I'm in the bottom! I'm in the bottom!' 'We know you're a bottom!'

2

Who said this about the mighty Crystal in season one?

'Crystal, my darling. How aptly named. Just like crystals, you are lifeless, stiff, and I can see right through you!'

3

Who said this about themselves in season two?

'I'm just all over the shop, really. I'm a bit of a mess... but a hot mess.'

4

Which of the gals threw this sassy shade at Baga?

'Baga looks like she's been dropped off from prison.'

5

Which of Ru's girls uttered these words?

'The cheek, the nerve, the gall, the gumption, the audacity!'

6

Which judge said this about one of the queen's efforts to look like Her Madge Elizabeth II?

'This is less Dame Helen Mirren and more DAMN! Helen Mirren.'

7

Which angry queen said this in Untucked?

'I'm going to tell you something right now girls. You underestimated me once, don't make the same mistake again.'

8

Which queen suggested that Lawrence do this with his RuPeter Badges:

'You can wear them as nipple tassles. One for each nip!'

9

Which of our girls said:

'I need a badge to prove myself to these other girls.'

10

Which queen said this about her magical drag transformation?

'I go from Gollum to gorgeous!'

11

Which queen uttered these immortal words?

'A red wig and a silver dress? I don't think.'

12

Which blink-and-you-miss-her queen boasted:

'I'm not a comedy queen. I'm not a performance queen. I'm not a look queen – I'm all of them.'

13

Which deadpan queen said this?

'Stick that in your death drop and shablam!'

14

Who said this to Cherry as soon as she entered the werkroom?

'Do they have good teeth in Darlington? No!'

15

Which queen described herself as:

'I'm a glamour Nana. I'm definitely a pig in a wig.'

'I do creepy drag to show the beauty in darkness.'

Charity Kase

Lancashire-born drag artist Charity Kase reveals why he loves Drag Race.

Halleloo for making it to *Drag Race* season three. As we can see, your drag is something else! How did you develop such a creative look?

I guess I've always been drawn to anything that's spooky or weird or on the dark side. I liked the constant change of creating new characters, new faces, new shapes and ideas of make-up. I didn't want to get stagnant with doing the same face and character every time.

Where did you grow up?

I grew up in Lancashire, in the Northwest, in a tiny little village in the middle of nowhere. It was very not me. I felt isolated. I felt different. I had a rough time in school. I was the only gay in the village. I lurked in the shadows as much as I could by hanging out in the art room at lunch or hanging out in the music room at break. But I would still wear pink buttons on my blazer and dye streaks in my hair. I liked standing out. I've always been someone who likes attention. That comes with the job as a drag queen. We love getting onstage and performing and making people happy and entertaining people.

So what was your audition tape like? It must've been quite extraordinary.

It was kinda crazy, actually. I was dressed as a creepy monster sat in the bath, shaving my legs with a really menacing razor.

What was it like walking into the werk room for the first time?

The whole first day was so surreal. It didn't feel like a real day. I mean, even now it still feels like it was a dream. It didn't feel like real life. Obviously, we're all running on adrenaline and we're all super nervous. It's easy to watch it and forget how nervous we were. We were all absolutely terrified.

What was your first catwalk like, walking down that runway and seeing Ru in her glamazon gear?

Now that put the fear of God into me, cos you're walking out onto the stage for the first time and there are so many lights and so many cameras and it's all a little intimidating.. And then you walk offstage thinking, 'Oh my God, I hope they liked that.' That was scary.

'I liked standing out. I've always been someone who likes attention.'

Why do you think it's so important that Victoria Scone is on the show?

Because Victoria's participation proves that drag is an art form that anybody can take part in. Lots and lots of AFAB people do. I love Victoria, she's incredible. Some of my favourite queens are AFAB queens. Some of my favourite queens are trans performers and drag kings. That's what being part of the LGBTQ+ community is about. It's about being equal.

The Queen of the Queens Quiz

How much do you know about Mama Ru
and her legendary show?

1. **What is RuPaul's full name?**

2. **Name RuPaul's first single**

3. **Which cosmetics brand did RuPaul sign to in the nineties?**

4. **Which British rock legend did RuPaul duet with in the nineties?**

5. **In 2018, RuPaul was the first drag queen to receive which honour?**

6. **Who did Sum Ting Wong play in the Snatch Game?**

7. **Name three films RuPaul has appeared in**

8. **Which music video did RuPaul star in before she was famous?**

9. **Which queen was eliminated twice in series 2?**

10. **Which countries launched a series of *Drag Race* in 2021?**

11. **What was the name of Baga and The Vivienne's spin-off TV show?**

12. **What was the second single by the Frock Destroyers called?**

13. **How many international series of *Drag Race* have there been?**

14. **Which US *Drag Race* star was on the judging panel of *Canada's Drag Race*?**

ANSWERS

1. RuPaul Andre Charles (all three names required). 2. 'Supermodel (You Better Work)'. ('We'll allow just 'Supermodel'.) 3. MAC Cosmetics, for the VIVA GLAM campaign. 4. Elton John. 5. A star on the Hollywood Walk of Fame. 6. David Attenborough. 7. Any three of the following: *To Wong Foo, Thanks for Everything! Julie Newmar* (1995), *The Brady Bunch Movie* (1995), *A Very Brady Sequel* (1996), *But I'm a Cheerleader* (1999), *Starrbooty* (2007), *Another Gay Sequel: Gays Gone Wild!* (2008) *Hurricane Bianca* (2016). 8. 'Love Shack' by The B-52's. 9. Joe Black. 10. *Drag Race España* in Spain and *RuPaul's Drag Race Down Under* in Australia and New Zealand. 11. *Morning T&T*. 12. 'Her Majesty'. 13. Eight: US, UK, Holland, Canada, Thailand, Australia/New Zealand (*RuPaul's Drag Race Down Under*), Spain (*Drag Race España*) and Chile (*The Switch*). (Half a point for seven of the countries.) 14. Brooke Lynn Hytes.

'Being the first AFAB
queen felt right!'

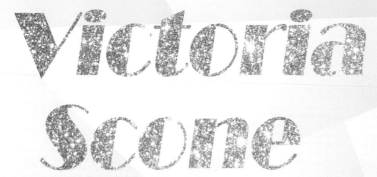

Victoria Scone

Meet the fabulous Cardiff-based Victoria Scone who makes Drag Race UK herstory by becoming the show's first ever AFAB (assigned female at birth) queen in season three.

Victoria, you are Drag Race UK's first ever AFAB queen. You must be thrilled, excited, nervous ...

When I auditioned for the show I was like, 'This feels absolutely right. This should be happening. You're meant to be there.' If it was going to be anyone, it was going to be me first.

What was it like finding out you would be joining the cast of season three?

Obviously I've been a massive fan of the show and of RuPaul since the beginning. It was only when I saw RuPaul standing in front of me that I finally believed I was on the show. I actually got a little bit emotional when I saw RuPaul – I didn't expect that I would. My throat was quivering a little bit.

What got you started?

Drag kind of embodies everything that I love and all the skills I'm good at. I love creating and I love sewing and I love singing. I just love entertaining. So it all accidentally came together in a big explosion of drag. My mum, who had been a Benny Hill girl in the 1970s, pushed me into the theatre. I loved it, but I went on a journey to get there.

In what way?

When I was younger, there was a period of time [when] I went to a dance school and was picked on because I was so slim and had what looked like a masculine figure, because I had a six pack. I gave up dance for a while and my weight went up and down. Then, when I decided to dance professionally, I went to multiple colleges and was told, 'You need to lose weight, you need to be this size to get in.'

That's certainly not fair.

Exactly. I knew I was talented and when I finally understood that my bodyshape really had nothing to do with it, that's when I thought, 'Oh, screw it'. I still got the lead role at the end-of-year show even though I wasn't skinny, and from then on I began to feel really good about myself. That's partly how I went on to become a drag queen. As I began to embrace my body shape, I entered a plus-size pageant for cis women and people identifying as female and I won it! After that, I wanted to try something else - I've rekindled my theatre background, and began to play around with make-up and characters and soon enough, Victoria Scone was born.

Your name is just brilliant. How did you choose it?

I originally came up with the name Victoria Sponge because I wanted something regal and royal and something very British – something to do with food because I'm a plus-size lady. And then I went with Scone because it's supposed to sound like, 'Where's Victoria? Oh, Victoria Scone,' but no one ever gets that. Ha!

How did the queens react to having an AFAB queen among them?

It was so welcoming when I walked in. There were huge cheers and whoops although I think even a couple didn't realise that I wasn't' the same gender as them!

'It was only when I saw RuPaul standing in front of me that I finally believed I was on the show.'

Before going into the series, were there any challenges you were nervous about?

I think I was relatively prepared for everything coming my way. I wasn't apprehensive about anything in particular before I went in – that's a very boring answer! I had prepared myself mentally for what we knew was coming, like the Snatch Game and the girl-band challenge. If you're not prepared, then what are you doing? I think I had put myself in a very good position.

Mini Challenge

You Better Word Search

If you can find all the words in the grid, shantay, you stay. If you can't, then sashay away!

```
M Y B Q Y S T B F S H A N T A Y I F N D
I Z D Y F U N I Q U E N E S S F S Z S S
S S I L M I C H E L L E V I S A G E H T
V C I X G S N S N A T C H G A M E H A U
E A H S G R Q A W C A W H O R A P T D C
A X T E S C A D Y E H D Q K S L A Y E K
V B T S R Y H H S C R E E L E G A N Z A
P G L R A R T A A H S K R A G B Z M S N
R M K U A S Y H R M Y I R Y T A F O T E
E O P Z H V H V A I N A J O L H G E G R
A R B T B Y A A A T S O A Q O H D G Q V
L T U I F S D G Y L W M R A M M O R R E
M A A P M I D R A A E A A T A C R L O N
E Y E D A I E I A N W N L V O S B T E P
S C Q O B U N R R N Z A T K B N C H P O
S E W V M N L I C J G A Y I W A E E A F
J C N R E A D O W E W E O J N I G T I A
R A L A N C A R R M F G A J W E B A N R
R C Z L D T R U P E T E R B A D G E T G
K T W K S I C K E N I N G V E H P M R N
```

RUPAUL	EXTRAVAGANZA	SHANTAY
MICHELLE VISAGE	FIERCE	SICKENING
ALAN CARR	GAG	SISSY THAT WALK
A'WHORA	GRAHAM NORTON	SLAY
BAGA	NERVE	THE T
BIMINI	PAINT	TAYCE
BLU HYDRANGEA	READ	TUCK
CHARISMA	REALNESS	UNIQUENESS
CHERRY VALENTINE	RUPETER BADGE	WERK ROOM
CHERYL HOLE	SASHAY AWAY	YAAAAS
DEATH DROP	SNATCH GAME	
ELEGANZA	SHADE